White Whale

A Novel

White Whale

A NOVEL

Robert Siegel

HarperSanFrancisco
An Imprint of HarperCollinsPublishers

HarperCollins Web Site: http://www.harpercollins.com

HarperCollins®, ▟ ®, and HarperSanFrancisco™ are trademarks of
HarperCollins Publishers Inc.

FIRST HARPERCOLLINS PAPERBACK EDITION PUBLISHED IN 1994
ISBN 0–06–251017–7 (pbk.)

An Earlier Edition of This Book Was Cataloged as Follows:

Siegel, Robert.
　　White whale : a novel / Robert Siegel. — 1st ed.
　　ISBN 0–06–250797–4
　　1. Whales — Fiction.　I. Title.
　PS3569.I382.W55　　1991
　813'.54—dc20　　　　　　　　　　　　　　　　90–84983

96　97　98　99　RRD(H)　10　9　8　7　6　5　4　3　2

For Ann,

Surely as the sun swims after the moon,
So does my heart press hard after yours.
Though my flukes fly as far as the Pole,
My soul sails to you as if to its center.

A Key to Pronouncing the Whale Names

The initial *H* is aspirated (pronounced in a breathy manner).

Hralekana:	hRA-LA-KA' NA
Aleea:	A-LEE' A
Hrūna:	hROO' NA
Lewtë:	LOO' TA
Hrunta:	hRUN' TA
Hreelëa:	hREE-LEE' A
Hrekka:	hREK' KA
Hrobo:	hRO' BO
Keeala:	KEE-A' LA
Bala:	BA' LA
Hrēta:	hREE' TA

White whale, you come
spindrift from the wave,
like a fish all white
and silver in the offing,
glimmer of the deep,
face of the moon,
ice at the world's end—
this word that I keep
trying to sing.

—Hrūna's Song

It was the same muffled, disembodied, and unearthly sound,
seeming to come from an immense distance: out of the sea,
out of the rocks around us, out of the air itself.

—Farley Mowat, in Mind in the Waters

He rises, a sudden white mountain
through the sea's green flanks marbled with foam
and beats the air with ghostly wings,
crashing on his back, spouting his music,
his eye wrinkled and wise . . .

—The Great Wing of New England

Prologue

I will now sing the tale to you as I sang it on the night of the gloria, a night when moonlight drenches the sea until the foaming crest of a wave is lost in the flashing trough and sparks above the waves vanish in the dazzle of the moon seen from below. While the moon transfigures sky and ocean, we whales rise from the waters like the primordial land itself in the beginning, dark and shining, to celebrate the freshness of first things—and things from these latter days. Our breath hangs above us in a mist as we blow, haloing the moon. Such a night calls forth our song, pulls it from our throats over the bright water, through the sweet tropic air of the islands.

From under the sea in chorus comes the low vibrato of the great bulls, the whistles and sharp cries of the yearling cows, the voices of the young males yearning to reach around the world; and then, lightly at first, as if from a great distance, a deep golden voice bringing all the world on its back, the ocean and the mountains and the sky. The voice mounts with the resonance of the coming dawn, rising toward the moon even as light pours from her, coating the waves and flashing in each eye.

While the one voice sings, other voices weave around it a harmony as profound and ancient as that between fire and water in the deepest trench of Ocean. Still others answer the echoes from the far caverns of the sea and the faint reverberations among the stars. And ever new light pours down, like the silent voice of the moon herself.

Even so was the night of the gloria when I, Hralekana, first sang my song from the beginning through my darkest hour—the song which I now sing for you.

Chapter One

I HRALEKANA-KOLUA, while I have time and breath, will sing my tale of the glory and the abyss—and of all things between that have filled my span of days.

I remember the night I was born, though some say that is impossible. My first memory is of struggling to move my flukes. Before that I recall nothing but a sense of serenity and a light difficult to describe. First, I felt my flukes and the cold ocean water. Later, my flippers broke free and I moved. I opened my eyes and saw light bending and swelling above me and I yearned toward it. Something rose under me and pushed toward the light, and in a moment I was above the water and saw the moon. I drew in air, let it out, and heard a high whistle, which I did not know was my own. I slapped the water with my flukes, and that was the second sound I heard. Next I saw a huge shadow under me and a white-and-black shape lying next to me and an even larger shape swimming in fast circles about me. There memory ends, for I fell asleep.

I don't know why I remember my birth when others say they do not remember theirs. But I believe we remember all that happens to us. Memory is like the deep ocean, and some plunge down farther into it than others. If I go far enough, I remember things from before my birth, things that I will not say here. Deep in that ocean, however, is the memory of feeding under the moon as a calf. I'd wake on the surface, where my mother held me up on her back, and slap my tail and skitter across it to plunge under her. She rolled over till her white belly shone like another moon, the water streaming in phosphorous bubbles from her flippers as she reached to steady me, her giant flukes fanning slowly up and down.

The milk came like a river of moonlight. I took it into myself in warm gulps, closing my eyes and opening them again. I was lost in this river, blue white on the waves. It filled and splashed over me and radiated out behind us. Bubbles of milk floated over me like stars the sun swallows when he leaps in the dawn.

Pressed to her warm belly, taking the milk into me, I felt the slow beat of her heart. And as I drank, she held me with her flippers and crooned:

> Around, over, and under the sea,
> Come, oh come, White Whale to me.
> The moon pursues her watery wish
> While stars are fleeing like herring fish.
> Soon day will come with the red-fluked dawn
> When all the starry fish are gone.
> Around, over, and under the sea,
> Come, oh come, White Whale to me.

I wondered who the white whale was that she sang about and thought it must be the moon, lazily swimming after the herring stars. Lying on my side feeding, I stared at the moon until my eyes closed. Sinking into darkness, I heard the slow beat of my mother's heart and her whole body hum with the melody she shared with the night.

Often my father Hrūna swam alongside, his hump cutting a black shadow against the moon and his wake bending like a bow of bright stars. Mounting from the ocean floor, his deep voice rose to support Mother's melody— looming over it like a dark island against which her song broke in a wild surf—before it receded again to the depths.

The mothers lay in that blissful tropical sea like so many floating islands around which swam calves like myself. Because I was born late in the year, all were larger than I and ventured from their mothers sooner. In the warm afternoons, while the mothers lolled in the shallow seas, the calves chased each other around the dozing islands of flesh or played by the reef and its forest of bright coral. I watched them from behind my mother's flipper.

I met the first of these playmates while taking an afternoon nap. My mother Lewtë dozed in the hot sun, and I lay stretched across her back, partly out of the water. *SSST*—spray in the eye woke me and a blowhole bobbed out of sight. I blinked, and a face rose up grinning and squirted my other eye. Whistling, I slipped off Lewtë's back. Coming up for air, I heard the smack of flukes on water and choked as the wave covered my blowhole.

A high, wild laugh faded toward the nearby reef. I was up and charging after it when my mother stopped me with her flipper.

"Don't mind that pest," she said, touching my face gently. "It's only Hrekka."

Over the next few days Hrekka repeated this trick so often the whole pod called him Hrekka the Pest. But the next time he tried it on me, I was waiting and threw myself at his blowhole the instant it appeared. This time it was he who choked and sputtered. I followed him past the nearby reef into the green waters of the lagoon. And Mother let me go.

Without a thought I left her safe shadow and followed Hrekka the Pest out into the world. Through the light green water, dancing with sunlight, the wall of coral loomed over me, pink and yellow and blue. Even as I watched Hrekka join the calves rolling and circling on the sandy bottom, I couldn't keep my eyes from the bright shapes that spired and twisted from that reef. Among them, darting and hanging, swam red, silver, and purple fish.

The other calves were moving in a circle-game accompanied by shrill whistles and squeals. I stopped, suddenly shy. There were five of them, all larger than I. Hrekka fixed one eye on me as he moved with the others, smirking. He stopped mid-circle and, waggling his flippers, called to the others, "Here comes the White Shrimp!" The four, all females, turned and stared. Two smiled behind their flippers. Without warning, Hrekka charged, butting me in the side. "Beluga!" he cried, "*Beluga,* what are you doing here with us *real* whales?"

I didn't know then what a Beluga was (a kind of whale a little larger than a dolphin and colored white). I thought it might be some sort of game. So I butted him back, gently. He laughed and swam backwards, ready to charge again, when one of the larger females swam between us.

"Leave him alone, Hrekka," she said, "or pick on someone your own size." She turned to me and smiled. Her flippers were all white, and she had a white streak down each side, like my mother. Her forehead was marked with a star.

"I'm Aleea—" she said, "short for Alaleea. What's your name?"

"Hralekana," I said and stopped, embarrassed. The others crowded around, blowing bubbles in spiral chains, never still. They giggled and rolled until Hrekka cried, "Air!" and all six of us raced to the top for a breath. Surfacing, we blew hard. Each tried to make the biggest spout. Hrekka blew a cloud of mist larger than his head, so I ducked down, came up, and put everything I had into it, squeezing my ribs and clenching my jaws. The warm breath made a cloud between me and the sun, forming a rainbow which hung there a second before blowing away.

"Beautiful!" Aleea shouted. Hrekka, however, was unimpressed. He swam over and slapped his flipper against mine.

"Well, Shrimp, so you can blow rainbow rings! I guess that makes you almost a whale." I didn't know what to say, so I dove, and the others followed me down. That was the last time Hrekka called me Shrimp.

From then on, I spent all day with my five friends. We played every kind of game, chasing and hiding among the hills and caves of the reef, the many-branched coral brilliant in the long sunlit hours, until the sun slanted red and our mothers whistled us back to food and sleep.

I came to know that the sea has many kinds of folk, most of them different from us and from each other. The big silver groupers moved slowly and stared, making faces as their gills waved in and out. Starfish of all colors crept along the underwater cliffs and seaweed forests. The barnacled giant clams proved shy and clapped shut at our approach. When I tried to peer through the crack in one's shell, it squirted sand in my eye. The flounders shimmied away over the bottom, while countless schools of other fish—all colors of the rainbow—opened to let us pass and closed seamlessly behind us.

I learned always to check out a cave before entering it; moray eels, with teeth too large for their mouths, were nasty to meet head-on. The big sea turtles lumbered by like mobile mossy rocks, showing an ancient indifference to young upstarts. I came to know countless varieties of anemones, the flowers of our underwater garden, and all manner of strange creatures who crept or scuttled along the bottom, such as the sea worms that swayed together in a dance like a forest of kelp moving in the tide.

Once, hiding in a cave, I disturbed a small octopus. He stared at me with mica-shiny eyes and flushed red and purple with anger as he oozed away on all eight legs.

Two fish our parents warned us about were jellyfish and stingrays. The transparent jellyfish were beautiful as they floated along in diaphanous clouds of all colors, looking wonderful to eat. But their dangling tentacles stung the mouth. The stingrays had long whiplike tails with spines that were even more painful. The grown-ups also told terrifying stories about sharks, especially the big white ones. They saw to it that none approached our lagoon.

One by one, the seemingly endless days passed. I grew faster than the others and soon was the largest in our group. I overheard Mother tell Father that I was taking more milk than any other calf. She smiled, and he made a funny kind of pleased grunt, looking up and down my length. No one made fun anymore of my being all white, though Hrekka remarked I must be growing into an iceberg.

None of us had seen icebergs, the white mountains that floated at the End of the World, where we would go to feed on krill once the waters warmed. The ice mountains shone white, green, or blue, depending on the light and, we were told, groaned and howled and sang as they bumped together in the polar ocean. Soon some of the grown-ups would leave early to scout our way there, to make sure it was clear of whalers.

Sometimes Lewtë and Hrūna left me and swam off under the moon. Once I watched them rise in the distance, white flippers extended like the wings of birds, and heard the thunderous clap as both hit the water at the same time.

On nights when the moon was too bright for anyone to sleep and drenched the waves in what is called a gloria, we were allowed to stay up and play in the center of a circle of adults. The grown-ups sang all night, and as their song swelled and ran back and forth under the waves, we calves leaped over each other, shouting and whistling and loudly smacking the water, our small noise drowned out by the great song of our elders.

On other nights we looked for a grown-up who liked to tell stories and heard all manner of things about whales, sky, and ocean, and about the strange islands and masses of land where we could never go. We often gathered around Lewtë or Hrūna, or my grandparents, Hrunta and Hreelëa, all of whom loved to tell stories—or sing them rather. For the speech of the Humpbacks is musical, and to weave sounds together artfully is as important to us as to tell the tale.

Lewtë told us of the beginning of all things, of how the Whale of Light swam alone in the Ocean of Light until, to share his joy, he spouted a great breath containing the sun and stars, the sky, the ocean, the land, and all creatures that swim, creep, or fly. She told us how each creature in some way resembled the one whose breath it was.

As we listened and dreamed in the shadow of the islands those moon-washed nights, Lewtë also sang of Ohobo the Hunter, whose loud voice spoke in the midst of storm and whose jagged harpoon lit up the sky. Woe to the whale caught on the surface by him! When the waves grew to silver gray mountains, the clouds roiling dark above them, and the foam flew so fast it stung the eyes, we'd dive for the bottom. Then Ohobo's jagged harpoon, sometimes white, sometimes red, danced harmlessly above us in its rage until the short tropical storm passed.

She told us that we whales need fear no animal in the sea nor on it—no animal, that is, except man and, while we were still young, the great white shark. Also, the Killer whale was not to be trusted, especially in ravenous packs. We should also beware of the giant squid. This last monster lurked in the Black Deep and was rarely seen. Nearly as large as a grown whale, squids had many long tentacles, some as big around as a palm tree, with which they trapped their prey. Their large, glassy eyes hid no kindness. At the center of their legs was a cruel beak with which they devoured their paralyzed victim. Our cousin the Sperm whale boldly hunted these monsters and engaged them in life-and-death struggles in the deep, which we celebrated in our songs. Many an old warrior Sperm whale had hundreds of scars on his body from the grip of those terrible tentacles.

I will never forget the night Lewtë told us the story of her rescue from men. I was already longer than the others (in the moonlight Hrekka called me the Blue Iceberg), but the six of us were still dwarfed by my mother as we lay in a half circle about her head, Aleea next to me. She told us of how one night while the pod slept, an iron monster with men on its back had caught her in a huge net and dragged her away.

At this point, Mother's voice trembled as she told how my father Hrūna, her childhood playmate, sensed she was in trouble and came halfway around the world to rescue her. Afterward Lewtë and Hrūna wove their songs together under the moon in the great and sacred wedding dance. Here her voice caught and she paused, while Aleea snuggled closer. Hrekka had fallen asleep, softly snoring while bubbles winked and burst over his blowhole.

That tale kept me dreaming for nights on end. It is difficult to say whose stories were more exciting. My father Hrūna told us of the many ages when whales lived without fear as lords of the ocean, before men began to hunt us in wooden monsters blown along by the wind. Still the whales throve, and their numbers did not diminish. Then within memory of our grandfathers, the humans came in larger monsters, made of iron, and hunted us down in merciless slaughter till the sea ran red with blood.

Nowadays the whale hunters were fewer, he said, but we whales were only one-tenth the number we had been. The great Blue whales were so few they might soon vanish, and the Sei and the Fin were sadly diminished. The noble Sperm whale, enemy of the giant squid, was still hunted without remorse, as were the lesser whales like the Minke and the Pilot. Meanwhile, thousands of dolphins and porpoises were murdered by humans greedy for tuna and other fish the dolphins ate.

Gone now were the great heroes of old, who had made war against the wooden monsters and sometimes with their flukes knocked harpooners into the ocean or with mighty heads stove in the timbers of whaling ships. The last and best of these had given his life trying to break the metal sides of the iron monsters with red and green eyes that scoured the ocean looking for our kind. Still, the last of the mighty had gone to a hero's death, taking one iron monster with him.

In the blue moonlight Hrūna's stories of these heroes both terrified and thrilled us, and we drew close under his shadow at the mention of the monsters. My heart raced, thinking of those mighty clashes between whale and monster, and I imagined myself charging the steel hide of one head-on and sending it to the bottom. (Hrekka and I made up a game in which we butted each other and whoever was the monster had to sink to the bottom.) But my heart grew sad at the thought that so many whales had perished. I also felt a kind of sadness that men had done this. I wondered about this bony animal that couldn't swim but moved on land upon its flukes, and about the monsters whose backs it rode over the sea, wreaking death upon its fellow creatures.

All of these things filled my dreams, but the story that made me feel as if the moon herself had lifted my heart on her flukes was that of the passing of Hralekana the Great, for I knew that I had been named after him and that his name meant White Whale.

My father told how Hralekana had lived many hundreds of years, now and then going forth to do battle with the wooden monsters. When the iron monsters replaced them, he stayed far below in his cavern somewhere between here and the End of the World. Not long after Hrūna had become leader, the pod was surprised by whalers. At that moment, Hralekana rose from the deep and charged the harpoon ships alone. So mighty was his onslaught that he sank one ship before he met his end. Singing his Death Song, he rolled and thrashed, tangling harpoon lines so that cow and calf could flee to safety. While they watched, the sea turned to blood around Hralekana, and the white whale spouted his bloody breath into the air, singing to the end. So by his death did the pod escape under the ice.

When he finished, everyone was silent. I felt I had to get away, and I swam out by myself on the glittering waves. My heart was so full it felt large as the moon. I swam until the moon, white as the great Hralekana himself, dipped her flukes under the horizon.

Chapter Two

ONE evening the pod gathered in the red light of the setting sun. My father spoke, saying he and five others—two bulls and three cows—were leaving to scout a safe route to the beds of krill by the Ice at the End of the World.

The pod woke early in the silver mists to see them off. Hrūna hugged me in his flippers and, eye to eye, told me to behave and to take care of Mother while he was away. That made me feel twice as large as I was, but when he turned to leave, I felt small again. Mother smiled to cheer me up, though she was sad too.

Aleea's father and the others joined him, and slowly they swam away. Gradually a low, sonorous chorus rose among the remaining pod. The volume climbed, and the rhythm quickened. It was the Song of Farewell:

> *Wherever on the waters the winds shall find you,*
> *Wherever the moon or the sun shall move,*
> *Hidden in the heavens or splendid high above you,*
> *Deep in my heart I will breathe deeply with you*
> *The breath of the one who made you and keeps you.*

This was the formal good-bye we used when Humpbacks parted for long. Ordinarily the song was shortened to "The breath of the one be with you" or "The breath of the one." When the last syllable trailed off, all six scouts rose in a magnificent leap, white flippers spread like wings, tinted in the coming dawn. In perfect formation they turned, flipped their tails, and landed on their backs.

A deep, rhythmic chant began, to which we calves kept time by smacking the water with our flukes. It was the Song of the Hunt:

> Guided by a star may you steer where they swim,
> The Leaping Whale lead you lightly on the way.
> May the herring swarm higher than the stars in heaven,
> May the krill run cold where they crowd the ocean.

While the grown-ups sang, the mist grew brighter around us. By now the scouts had disappeared from sight. The smells of sea and land mingled, fresh in the growing dawn. I had never been up so early and thought then, as since, that sunrise is the best moment of the day. Still the song ascended into the brightening air, and I understood the saying among us, "Morning is gold in the mouth."

When the sun cleared the mist, we calves scuttled off to play. At our age, the weeks the scouts were gone seemed like years, and each day stretched endless with adventure in those green and golden seas. Called home by Lewtë as the moon rose, feeling deliciously weary, I fell asleep at her side while feeding. Even as I drifted off, I felt the vibration of her bones as in her depths began the Song of Distant Love.

This was not a song lamenting the absence of my father, but one she sang to him. For sound travels great distances underwater along the canyons on the ocean floor and may be heard hundreds, even thousands, of miles away. It's possible that the song of a Humpback whale can be heard halfway around the world. So it was that my mother sang to my father and hoped that the sound reached his ears:

> Now, my Love, while the waves shine whitely,
> Each to each in the moon's bright leap,
> My song goes searching till your song shall answer—
> Its word come back with the wandering wind.
> All night as the white moon swims over the sea,
> The light of the sun finds her in the heavens;
> So does my love shine for you surely,
> Whatever black deep or dark you are daring.

Afterwards she listened through the night, hoping to catch, hours later, the faint strains of his response. While she patiently waited, I slept, but now and then she'd wake me to listen with her. Then I might hear, as faint as surf on a distant shore and hard to distinguish from the myriad sounds of the sea, the voice of my father singing:

> Surely as the sun swims after the moon,
> So does my heart press hard after yours.
> Though my flukes fly as far as the Pole,
> My soul sails to you as if to its center.

Sometimes the throb of a distant ship's propeller drowned the words, but my mother said that she knew what they were anyway. When I asked how, she smiled and said, "One heart, one mind."

The calves' games grew more elaborate in the lagoon. After a while, we'd explored nearly all of it. One day we found a narrow inlet on the side our parents didn't watch. We kept this inlet a secret among us, and now and then dared each other to go through it into the Blue Deep beyond.

One day Aleea and I left by that inlet, determined to explore the floor of the ocean, which there fell off deeper than we'd ever gone before. The water was colder too, and the surface more violent than we were used to. A chill passed through me as we left the lagoon, but I said nothing to Aleea.

A half mile out from the reef we took a deep breath and dove. Quickly we plunged through the rays of sun in the Green Deep, down into the mysterious Blue, where everything shone dim. Below us the tops of giant seaweed swayed back and forth in the current, and when we reached the first fronds, we paused. We both had been warned not to become tangled in it.

"Are you sure you want to go deeper?" I asked Aleea.

"Let's see what's down there," she said, her voice higher than usual. "We can always come back up."

As we squeezed between the moving fronds of the weeds, some as tall as palm trees on the islands, we felt them run over our skin like hundreds of tiny flippers— back and forth, back and forth, as if measuring us. We shivered. Farther down the fronds disappeared, and we swam between smooth stems as thick as tree trunks and bending like palms in a storm.

At the bottom giant clams, crusted with sea lice and barnacles, lay half open, waiting for whatever the current might bring. They were larger than those in the lagoon, and we steered carefully between them, not wanting to lose a flipper or a fluke. We wove among the bending stems for a long time until they thinned out where the ocean floor sloped down to darkness.

When we rose for air, the island was a surprising distance away, a white line of surf with a few tiny palms sticking above it. My stomach felt queasy, and I knew we should return but said nothing in case Aleea would think I was afraid. Silent, we went down again.

The floor dropped off beyond the giant weeds, and we followed the slope down. Soon we saw two dark shapes in the twilit water. At first we thought they were whales, but they loomed too large for whales. Both lay still, like rock, covered with grayish moss and plants, one a mile beyond the other. Cautiously we approached the first, stopping a distance from it. The silence was unbearable.

At last, to break it (and, I confess, to show off), I yelled and charged the huge thing. I butted it head-on, and some weed came away. Underneath was something like the logs that floated in the lagoon. It was wood. Not to be outdone, Aleea roared and butted it too. She laughed a high, silvery laugh, and we both felt brave.

"Do you think this is one of the wooden ship-monsters Hrūna told us about—only *dead?*" I asked. At the word *dead* we backed up and looked around. Nothing happened, but the word hung there in the eerie silence. Cautiously we

21

swam up the side to the monster's back, wondering if we would find drowned humans there. Its back was flat, but higher at both ends. There was nothing on it except weeds and big logs broken off at the roots like trees in a typhoon. Along the sides were holes where the monster's eyes had been. Out of some poked round black iron things like the eyes on goby fish, but these had no life in them. Everything was covered with moss, which came off when brushed by a flipper. Some of the wood crumbled too.

The deck of the wooden monster slanted, and we swam up it and over the opposite side. Both of us whistled, for on that side a hole stretched from top to bottom. Larger than the two of us, it gaped like a dark mouth. Still the monster was dead and the humans gone, and I felt a terrible curiosity to see what was inside.

Slowly we edged in half a flipper length, then a half more, until our eyes adjusted to the gloom. This was the monster's stomach all right. Big wooden ribs curved down into the sand. The belly was empty and large enough for us to swim side by side from one end to the other around tree trunks that grew up through the backbone—the same ones we saw broken off on top. It was empty except for mounds of sand covered with sea worms and algae.

Aleea brushed the sand from a mound. Under it lay a long thin bone and a round bone—round as a dolphin's forehead—with three holes in it and teeth.

"A dolphin's?" she asked, "or—"

"Or a *human's*," I whispered. We shuddered and covered it again.

Gingerly with my flipper I fanned the top of the biggest mound. Sand and moss flew up and blinded me a moment. Underneath lay crumbling wood, old and soft. I touched it, and as the wood gave way, something bright flashed underneath. Even in that dim light things glimmered yellow in a pile. They were big as pebbles, smooth pebbles on the beach, with larger objects among them shaped like starfish or coral branches. Stones of different colors stuck to these.

I thought they might be good to eat and scooped several in my mouth. But they lay heavy and rocklike on my tongue, and I spat them out on the sand.

"Let's go," I said to Aleea. "We can't eat these." But she stared at them, her eyes shining.

"Wait. I have an idea," she said. "Let's take these in our mouths and carry them back to the reef where we can look at them in the light." So we each took a mouthful of the cold, hard objects and, careful not to swallow any, left the dead monster and swam up the long blue slope to the green shallows by the reef. On a patch of white bottom sand not far from the secret inlet, we emptied our mouths.

We were hardly prepared for what we saw. The yellow pebbles and bars glittered brighter than a cloud of flying fish, and the flashing stones blazed in the sunlight like fires on the island at night. These were all colors—red, green, blue, purple, yellow, and brilliant white. We wondered if they were the wooden monster's glowing eyes that we had heard about. Aleea moved them around with her flipper and lifted one bunch that hung together like a strand of seaweed. From the end dangled and flashed a stone-encrusted object shaped like a starfish. She waved it about in the water until the strand became stuck on her flipper, and I had to pull it off with my mouth.

"Let's show them to our friends," I said.

Aleea didn't answer. "No," she said at last. "These are ours. We found them. Let's keep them as our secret—yours and mine only." There was a new look in her eye. I thought the idea strange but reluctantly agreed.

"All right," I said. "They'll be our secret."

"And the ship-monster too?"

"And the monster too," I promised.

At that moment we heard a triumphant yell and turned to see Hrekka speeding out of the lagoon.

"Quick, hide them," Aleea said, and bellied down to the sand, waggling her flippers till all the yellow pebbles and bright stones were covered.

"What are you two up to?" asked Hrekka, looping about us a bright chain of bubbles. "We've been looking for you everywhere."

"Exploring—and we're not going to tell *you* where," Aleea said, swimming off toward the inlet where the others were waiting.

While we played that afternoon, Aleea's mind was elsewhere. I wanted to show the others the wooden monster, but I didn't betray our secret. The secret made me feel uncomfortable, as if I were two whales.

24

Chapter Three

THE next day, as soon as we could get away, we returned to the outer reef.

"I think they're here, by the red coral," Aleea said, bellying down to the sand and making it fly. But flail as she might, no shining pebbles appeared.

"Maybe they're over here," I guessed and started to brush the sand. But they were not, nor in a dozen other places we tried. We left holes all over the white sand bottom. I thought Aleea was going to cry.

"Don't be sad," I said. "We'll get more at the broken ship."

We returned down the long slope into the Blue Deep where the two shadows waited. As we swam around the stern of the wooden monster, the dark eyes in its tail stared down at us. The same prickly feeling as yesterday moved down my spine. In the dark belly we cleared away the sand that had covered the mound overnight. The sight of the pebbles pushed all misgivings from my mind. Excited, we bellied down and soon uncovered a huge quantity of the pebbles and bars—more than the two of us could carry.

"Before we take these back, let's look at the other ship-monster," I suggested. The second ship, an immense shadow, lay a distance down the slope. We breathed once at the surface and descended toward it. It was farther than it first looked and was at least three times as long as the other and twice its height. A small mountain rose on its back and hundreds of dark eyes stared down at us. From parts of the deck giant seaweed waved back and forth—beckoning to us, or warning us, like sea snakes ready to strike. Again the old feeling crawled down my spine, and my stomach tightened. If I hadn't been too proud, I'd have fled.

We swam up to the long gray side that would dwarf a grown-up whale. The monster was as large as an island. I touched its hide with my flipper and something reddish clouded the water. I touched it again, and it didn't feel like wood. It was scaly and hard. I struck it with my flukes and was immediately sorry.

BOOM—the side of the ship-monster resounded. *BOOM BOOM boom*—the echoes trailed off along its length, through its hollow stomachs, and returned again from the reef above—*boom* BOOM BOOM!

"What's *that*?" Aleea asked, bumping against me.

"Nothing," I said, resisting an urge to bolt. "It's only an echo. This monster's dead too. The hide is not wood, but iron. Remember, Hrūna told us how the waves bang and boom against the iron monsters, and how the ocean vibrates when they pass? That's the iron." Reassured by my own words, I struck it again.

While the echoes faded, we swam up and explored the top. Many blank eyes stared at us as we swam the length of the deck. We found no wooden logs, but iron ones, both fore and aft, mounted three above three, sticking out at an angle from the iron mountain. Each of these logs, hollow in the middle, was longer than I. I wondered if their hollow iron mouths spat the fiery serpents that bit whales.

I crossed to the other side, looked out over the ocean bottom, and nearly lost my breath. From this side I could see shadow after shadow of these iron monsters receding into the distance. Some were smaller, some larger, but all were dead. Of some only half remained, standing on end or turned upside down and twisted. Many had gaping holes in deck or belly, and the big iron logs and mountain of eyes were gone.

Then I saw what I had never seen before, and what I did not then understand. It was a picture inside my head, only more brilliant, and I knew that it was happening somewhere outside me. It was the first of the Seeings that have come ever more frequently as the years pass.

The picture showed the island in the gray morning mist. All the iron monsters were floating on the surface, and none was broken. Great flashes of red flame rose from the hollow iron logs and lit the sky like the harpoon of Ohobo. The noise was deafening, and the sea shook. In the distance other flashes showed the silhouettes of more iron monsters. From these also flames streaked, and all around the ships plumes of water exploded high into the air. Then a huge explosion shook one of the ships (the very ship we had found) and filled it with fire. There was shouting and screaming, and hundreds of short creatures with divided flukes leaped from the burning deck into the water. But the water itself was on fire, and I heard cries

29

until the flames stopped them. The other ships' mouths kept belching flames, even after they'd been struck by the flames from the distant ships. Giant birds swooped down at them, dropping fire as they droned and passed. The ships spat small flames at these birds, and sometimes one disappeared with a deafening noise in a ball of fire. The seas shone red as blood in the flames, and the iron logs slowly ceased to speak, for soon all the seas were burning. With a shudder through its whole length and a moan from the men, the ship under us sank, the white water rushing in as it settled to the deep. One by one the other ships sank. It grew dark and cold, and the bitter smell of burning and death hung in the air.

The picture faded, and once again I saw before me, very still, the ship graveyard. I sank down on the deck for a moment. Aleea looked at me, afraid. Then without a word, I moved on. We swam down the far side and found a gaping hole like the one in the wooden ship. Something large had made the hole, and the edges were jagged.

We stared through it into the darkness, trying to get our courage up. After my Seeing, the hole reminded me of death, and I felt we should leave. But Aleea whispered, "This monster's huge. I bet it has a bigger pile of yellow pebbles."

So, carefully avoiding the jagged edges of iron, we edged into the dark. We could barely see.

"Ah," I called loudly into the dark belly.

"*Ah Ah Ah*," sounded the echo, fading into the dim interior and returning as a whisper.

"There are many openings in here—many bellies," Aleea said, repeating what the echoes had told us. We slid through the hole. It was too dark in this ship's stomach, and we knew we shouldn't go in far. Near the entrance lay rows of round things like giant coconuts, only with spines like a sea urchin's sticking out of them. By these lay more bones, including three of the round ones staring with hollow eyes.

My stomach felt queasy. Beyond the bones it was so dark we explored by echo alone. We found many large wooden things piled on top of one another, but nothing that fell apart at a touch as in the other ship. In the dark all I could see was the dim star on Aleea's forehead.

"Ah," I whispered, and the echo told me that beyond the pile of wooden things a hole opened into another belly.

"Let's leave," Aleea said behind me in a small voice, just as I'd decided to explore it.

"No, wait a minute. I want to look into the next belly."

We swam around the wooden pile and came up to the opening.

"Ah," I called. No echo returned. That was strange. A moment ago the opening had echoed. Something must be blocking it after all. Confused, I turned back toward the dim light of the hole, farther off than I remembered. Without a word Aleea turned too.

"SSS"—something behind us moved. I heard it lightly brush the floor. A snake wriggled across the dim light in front of me. At least I thought it was a snake. At the same instant I felt something tickle my side, the whole length, and cross my back. Glancing sideways I saw a snake arch over Aleea and wrap itself around her.

"Alee—" I started to warn her, when sharp pains seized me in a dozen places and squeezed my belly in a noose.

"Aleea!" I shouted as I saw her twist wildly. For a moment everything was confused. I thrashed and struggled toward the hole, pulling with all my might, and felt a second snakelike thing wrap around me. I banged against the wall of the ship's stomach, and clouds of rust blinded me. Aleea squealed in pain.

For a long minute I felt paralyzed, stuck. Then something behind gave way, and by luck I flopped through the hole, Aleea behind me wriggling like a flounder. Around her writhed giant snakes. They flew in front of me and I bit down as hard as I could and got a piece of one in my mouth.

In the grip of whatever it was, I twisted and looked back. From the hole slid a pale, bloated body with glittering eyes, waving many legs, thick as palm trees and tapering out to snakelike tips. Each leg was studded with suction cups, and two legs already tightened around each of us. In the middle of all these legs a sharp black beak opened and closed.

It was the giant squid.

With every ounce of strength in my flukes, I jerked toward the surface far above. Aleea pulled too, like a crippled flounder, while the tentacles slowly, leisurely rolled about her, pulling her cup by cup closer to the clacking beak. The squid rolled us closer to its mouth as we dragged its enormous bulk up from the ocean floor.

Lungs bursting, I screamed louder than ever, hoping our mothers would hear. But they were on the far side of the island and had no idea where we were. My breath was gone, and spots flitted before my eyes. I saw Aleea, wrapped in three tentacles, cease to struggle as her cry stopped.

Clack, clack—the jaws snapped closer. A shadow passed over me, and I thought this was the end. A blur of bright days streamed past, and I felt foolish for having gone into the ship. Faintly I heard the war blast of an angry whale, and everything went dark.

It was really dark—but my lungs ached, and I realized I was still conscious. The water had turned black. I heard the war cry on top of me and a thump knocked out my remaining breath. Suffocating, I was pressed tight with slimy legs and a sharp pain pierced my flukes. I twitched once, twice, three times, and was suddenly free in the darkness. There was a thrashing of bodies about me and a horrible stench and suffocation. Then the black thinned out, and with a kick of my flukes I was in green water by a tremendous cloud of murk. Another kick brought me to the surface, where I gasped and floated limp. The sea in front of me boiled and seethed in a dark mass of bubbles and strange cries. Suddenly Aleea popped up out of it. She lay glassy-eyed and motionless, and I swam over and pushed her to the clear water.

"Aleea," I cried. "Aleea, can you hear me?" She lay low in the water, about to sink, pale and still. I plunged under her and held her up. She was cold to the touch and stiff.

"Aleea," I choked.

Her head above the waves, she at last made a noise, and water came rushing from her blowhole. Weakly she moved her flukes and inhaled. I was overjoyed, and tears came as I laughed with relief.

A few yards from us, the dark water boiled as cries of pain and trumpets of anger increased. Far in the distance we saw grown-ups speeding toward us. In the thrashing water something bulbous and light-colored rose up, and I recognized the staring eyes. Giant flukes made a mighty splash, and the squid sank again. With a rush of foam, a bull whale breached half out of water, wound about with the legs of the squid so that only his head was visible. But I knew the face and the one free flipper and yelled as loud as I could.

"Father!" Somehow Hrūna had found us. I saw other grown-ups approaching and recognized the five who had gone with him scouting for krill. They trumpeted and came on full speed. Returning to the pod, they had fortunately heard our cries.

Now neither party in this life-and-death struggle appeared. The surface boiled and, just as the others arrived, grew still. There were no more gutteral growls, cries of pain or *clack, clack* of the squid's beak, just an awful stillness in which the inky cloud grew larger and thinner and the surface oily calm. For a long minute no one moved or said a word.

Then legs like a mass of snakes flew up into the air, followed by the bulbous body of the squid with its staring eyes. Under it the body of Hrūna, belly up, wrapped in the tentacles, rose above the surface and lay still. A moan went up from the onlookers.

The two locked figures lay bobbing on the little waves.

At last Hrūna rolled over and let out the longest blow I have ever heard. The others cheered. The squid's eyes stared emptily, as one by one its tentacles unwound from Hrūna's body and floated lifeless on the surface. Where each disk had stuck there was a round mark on his skin and a little blood, so tight had been its hold. At that sight, I noticed the salt stinging in my own scratches. There was a foul taste in my mouth, and I realized I still clenched in my jaws the piece of tentacle I'd bitten off.

"Phooff! PHOOFF!" I spat it out, and it spiraled pinkly into the Deep.

Hrūna swam up to Aleea and me. "Are you two all right?" he asked anxiously, checking us from stem to stern.

"Yes," we said. "Yes!"

He looked relieved, then frowned. "What were you doing here so far from the pod?"

Father's expression was grave as we told our story, not without a lot of pauses, throat clearing, and passing of it back and forth. Fortunately, before we finished we were interrupted by a high squeal as Hrekka and the others found us and rollicked in to greet the grown-ups, jumping over their backs and splashing everyone, including the dead squid. A moment later, grunts and bellows, clickings and whistles announced that the rest of the pod was close behind.

Great was the celebration for the safe return of the scouts, for Hrūna's triumph over the giant squid, and for his rescue of Aleea and myself. Everyone was awed by Hrūna's victory. Only the toothed Sperm whale was known to do deadly combat with the frightening mollusk. Several of Hrūna's baleen plates had been broken, and he would bear the marks of the giant tentacles for the rest of his life. But as more than one said, they were scars to be worn proudly. The round disk marks on Aleea and myself, Lewtë told us, would soon go away, for our skin was young and growing. Aleea felt relieved, but I was disappointed. After all, hadn't I torn the tip off a monstrous tentacle?

How the squid had grown so large in these waters and what it fed upon in the belly of the ship were questions that none asked without a shudder.

That night under bright stars and the moon's narrow flukes we heard the news from the scouts. All six related what they'd seen on their journey. Without mishap, they'd reached the great krill beds where these spread to the horizon in all directions, sometimes to the depth of a mile, and color the ocean orange. Returning, they'd met a pod of Sei whales fleeing from whalers on the other side of the Pole. The fleet was smaller this year, but the Sei warned of pirate whalers who, like lonely sharks, prowled and fed on what they could find. Still our own way to the beds was clear. And the krill this year lay close to the refuge of the ice.

At such good news we sang, as we traditionally did, the Song of the Krill. Beginning with the low grunts and snorts of a single bull, the song swelled with deep voices like the voice of Ocean itself. The cows added silvery trills, imitating the light leaping of the krill:

> Broad is the krill, as far as we can follow,
> Deep it is, down to the depth of a mile,
> Crisp and sweet where it colors the ocean.
> O swift is the swimming and sweet is the swallowing,
> Wide is my mouth, and huge my joy,
> Lost in the midst of it, millions around me.

The words made me ravenous. They were followed by a new song composed that very day by Hrobo, the oldest bull in the pod, to celebrate Hrūna's slaying of the giant squid. His voice crusty as the barnacles that covered his face, Hrobo sang the Song of the Squid:

> Dark in the man-monster lay the great mollusk,

he began in a low, eerie tone, and Aleea shivered up close to me. He described how the squid had come upon the ship shortly after the sea battle and lain there for years, its pale bulk growing in the darkness while it fed on the unnameable. His voice rising with excitement, he described how Aleea and I accidentally woke it,

> in the baleful belly,
> In the iron ship's maw where so many were murdered.
> At that, the long limbs like a creeper came crawling,
> Sneaking like snakes through the slithery dark
> And grabbed them, surely, girl-calf and boy-calf,
> Clacking its beak as it boiled to bite them.

My heart swelled as he related how we had resisted it with all our strength,

> Whalefully they struggled against the strangler,
> Biting off a tip, never yielding to terror,

until Hrūna heard our cries and swam to our rescue:

> Still it coiled round them, clinging closer and closer—
> Till Hrūna bellowed loud and bore into the beast,
> Biting and flailing with his giant flukes.

The battle joined, the two were equally matched, and it looked as if Hrūna might be suffocated when the squid made

> muddy the deep with malevolent murk.

But finally Father emerged, scarred but triumphant:

> He struck and he bit like the heroes we've heard of
> And crushed the cruel squid till it squeezed no more.
> The hundred-snaked hydra lay limp in the daylight,
> Dreaded no more by dwellers of the Deep.

Hrobo closed, and there was silence. I was so pleased by that song, I smacked the water and whistled. Especially by the line, *Biting off the tip of one, not yielding to terror.* He had noticed. Someone had noticed what Aleea and I had done! *Whalefully*—he had used the word *whalefully* of us—

> Whalefully they struggled against the strangler.

I felt I was going to burst, so I dove deep until I had control of myself.

I thought how wonderful song was. Now that we had the day in song, not only would we not forget it, but we could relive it over and over. In song Hrūna would always rescue us, and in song we would always be brave and struggle whalefully.

After all had congratulated old Hrobo on his day's work, they joined in the traditional Salute to the Stars:

> The stars swim above us, shining and still,
> Herring fish steering high through the heavens,
> Following the endless path of the spray
> The Great Flukes fling in their far leaping—
> Countless, innumerable as the krill,
> School that circles a summer's night,
> Mist that blows from a bright breathing,
> Words dropped into an abyss of light.

While the last strains spooled out over the waters, I rocked to sleep on my mother's breast.

The next morning as the sun rose red in the east, we began a day of games. Both grown-ups and calves played breaching games to see who could leap the highest and turn the most flips or rolls in the air. Teams leaped together in formation, white wings stretched wide, white bellies glistening in the sun. A few performed a series of leaps up the glittering track of the rising sun—called a Sunward Journey—in which the spray rose golden, and it looked as if the leaper disappeared into the disk of the sun.

This feat was a rare accomplishment and received a thunder of flukes striking the surface.

The pod also played to see who could slap the water in the most intricate patterns of sound. We played at diving the deepest and singing the most uproariously and ended with the great Rollover—a weaving chain of leaps and splashes where the pod wove a white wake of water, leaping over each other for miles while singing in symphony.

This part we calves enjoyed the most, and the adults knew how to avoid landing on top of us. While they were resting, we continued our play, leaping over them and sliding down the long curved backs into the water. The grown-ups added a new trick this time. As I slid down Hrūna's back toward his flukes, he wrapped them around me and flipped me through the air far over his head. I was flying, my flippers guiding me like the wings of a bird. It is a feeling I recall to this day.

Physically tired, in the evening we made up new songs to old words and new words to old songs, and, of course, we told stories. These lasted late into the night until the last players fell asleep.

The next morning Hrūna called a Council of the Elders, and they asked Aleea and me to lead them to the ship-monsters' graveyard. In the presence of the pod, the wooden monster appeared smaller and not at all alarming. Lewtë helped us carry some of the shining pebbles to shallow water. All gazed at the glittering stones, and Aleea's mother, Keeala, spoke.

"I have seen such stones when I was a calf. They glittered then as now. I soon learned they could not be eaten and were good only to look at. At first I wanted to keep the ones I saw, though I did not know how. They were not part of me, like my flippers or flukes or eyes. They kept sinking under the sand. Also, unlike fish they did not move, so that I could not see them in many places, but only in one. When I looked at a school of the yellow and purple fish, followed by the blue and the red weaving among the coral, I realized that all around me flashed the same colors as in the cold, hard stones. And the fish were living and moving. If I wanted colors that stayed in one place, I could always visit the garden of anemones in the reef and find brilliant ones. I rose to the top of the sea and saw a rainbow and the sun streaming down, and I knew it was a true thing that I thought."

Everyone was silent as we swam down toward the larger ship where Aleea and I had disturbed the squid. I felt fear at the memory but went right up to the opening with Hrūna. The pod also explored the iron mountain and iron logs on top. They were silent as they looked over the many wrecked ships on the ocean floor. I recalled my vision of the flames but said nothing.

"So," Hrūna said at last, turning over one of the round bones, "it is as the dolphins told me. The human creatures destroy one another even as they destroy whales." He shook his head. "What kind of creature is it that kills its own kind?"

With a gravelly voice, Hrunta spoke up. "When I was a calf on the Lonely Cruise, one night I was awakened by what I thought was Ohobo's Harpoon. I saw a brightness in the sky that did not go away, and there was no storm. I swam toward it, though the noise was as deafening as thunder and shook the water.

"Morning had come by the time I neared the island. It was all covered with smoke. I saw iron monsters throwing fire at the island and the mountain on the island throwing fire back. Two of the ship-monsters were burning but still spitting flame.

"Near the shore and on the beach I saw thousands of the twin-fluked human kind. Many were in small ships that crawled toward the shore like crabs or lobsters, making much noise. At the shore these opened their mouths, and the men poured out along the beach. There must have been thousands. They crawled up the beach, where many lay still. But the ships kept throwing flames and making thunder. And sticks in the mens' flippers made fire and noise. Flames spitting from the mountain knocked the men down. Hundreds died in the water before they came to shore, and the water was red with their blood. Sharks gathered offshore.

"Sickened, I moved away from those bloody waters, but the scent is still in my blowhole, and the many cries of pain and anguish have entered into my song."

Chapter Four

T HE next morning the pod left its winter nesting grounds for the journey to the polar seas and the Ice at the End of the World. We calves were excited at the prospect, although sad to leave the lagoon and the bright waters of our infancy. Sun glittered on the green waves as we left the islands, gulls swooping and screaming good-bye above us. Calves and mothers swam in the center, ringed by the larger bulls and cows on the lookout for whalers, packs of Killer whales, and the occasional great white shark.

Every few days we'd stop to feed if we found a school of herring—next to krill, the Humpbacks' favorite food. The grown-ups worked together to catch them in bubble nets. They circled around the school, releasing bubbles in tighter and tighter rings. The herring drew together in a cluster and were easy to catch.

Aleea and I watched this herring hunt with fascination. I had never tasted herring before, but they looked good— each like a little star. I swam up to a bubble net and opened my mouth wide—but too soon—and got nothing but a mouthful of salt water. Lewtë showed me how to move right into the cluster, and the next time a few of the slippery fish stayed in when I shut my mouth and pressed the water out with my tongue. That first taste was sweet and delicate, and I have never forgotten it.

One night as we approached a low, rocky island we were greeted by a chorus of barks. It looked as if rocks on the island wriggled off into the sea. A moment later small black creatures circled, spiraled, and looped around us, yelping and slapping their flippers. They made me dizzy.

"Sea lions," Lewtë said, smiling, just as one considerably gray, with a white mustache, popped up in front of Grandfather Hrunta. Siloa the sea lion was his old friend, and there was jubilation at this reunion. Years before, when my father was a calf, Hrunta had saved two of the sea lion pups from a white shark.

We didn't get much sleep that night, for the sea lions feasted us with flounders and other delicacies. Rising in the moonlight with these in their mouths, water twinkling from their whiskers, they tossed them back and forth with many raucous barks and much applause before flipping them into the open mouth of a whale. In his excitement one sea lion pup fell into Hrunta's mouth and started screaming. Gently my grandfather raised his tongue until the youngster could wriggle over his baleen back into the water. At that, the sea quaked with whale laughter and the hilarious barks of his elders.

When we'd eaten, the whole pack tickled the calves, swimming close and slapping us with their flippers until we were weak with laughter. In return we let them hold on to us while we spun in the deep or flew through the air, two or three sea lions clinging by their teeth to each flipper.

They were just the first of many tribes of sea creatures we met on our way to the Pole. Two days later we heard faint whistles and clicks and saw a crowd of small bodies speeding toward us from the horizon, leaping and flashing in the air. These sleek and dazzling creatures swam and spoke even faster than the sea lions, and four popped up in front of Hrūna, foreheads glistening in the sun and all talking at once.

"Delphi, Marmo, Scallop, and Whitefin," Hrūna introduced them when for a moment they stopped chattering. They were Bottle-nosed dolphins, distant cousins of ours. Most were blue above and light below, with long, thin noses and bulging foreheads. Whitefin was all white like me, and Marmo, marbled white and blue. Hrūna had met them on his Lonely Cruise and had rescued Marmo and Scallop from the city of men. The pod gathered around to hear news of all the oceans, for the dolphins as usual were great gossips and knew everything that was going on.

They told us that the way to the Pole was still clear. The whaling fleet had not yet appeared by the krill beds, but pirate whalers were on the prowl. Halfway around the world one of the giant ship-monsters had sunk and spread a thick black poison over miles of sea. Many fish had died, and the dolphins saw gulls floating coated with the stuff. Some in our pod had never heard of such a thing happening before, and there were many grim words and grave faces.

All the time he was talking, Whitefin kept glancing at me. When Marmo took over the conversation, Whitefin swam up and squeaked in my ear: "Hralekana, I see it is your fate, like mine, to be all white. That is good."

47

He paused and looked pensive. "Never let it trouble you. The clouds are white, the ice is white, and white is the heart of the sun." He poked me with that thin nose of his and flashed away. His words sounded strange to me at the time, but later I often thought back on them with gratitude.

Before we left the warm waters behind, we came to the Waste Ocean. This was an eerie place, and the grown-ups grew silent. Life there had suddenly disappeared from the ocean bottom, and now no creature swam in the waters above it. The pod had to travel many leagues around it. We skirted the edge where the the seaweed gave out. On one side the coral reefs lay dead, while on the other they were filled with living animals and plants. When we had swum a whole day along this border, Hrūna told me the story as he'd heard it long ago from the dolphins.

Once there was an atoll like hundreds of other islands in this part of the ocean. Men had gone there on ships to build something and then sailed away. Without warning, a huge ball of fire appeared above the atoll, visible for a hundred miles. Then the tallest cloud anyone could remember rose miles above the island, dropping smoke and ashes. When the cloud moved away, the island had disappeared, together with all the creatures on it and around it. Foolish animals who swam toward the cloud to see what had happened sickened and died. Wise ones swam as fast as they could away from the island, for the great cloud spread over the sea in all directions, dropping ashes and dust mixed with rain. The waters grew deadly and all life died, including seaweed and the little coral polyps. For many years the surrounding ocean had remained this way—a dead place where no life would grow. Only recently had a few of the tougher sea plants begun to grow back.

"It is," Hrūna said to me that night, his eye close to mine, "the greatest evil humans have brought upon the ocean—that fireball. No one knows why they made it, for they didn't take the fish it killed. It is a worse evil than the oily poison that escapes when one of their giant ships breaks apart."

That night I couldn't sleep, so without telling a soul, I swam back to the edge of the Waste. I looked into its bare reaches, the bottom glimmering bone-white in the moon. I felt great sadness and fear, though no sense of personal danger. I felt some awful power threatening the ocean. It was then I had the second of the Seeings that have come to me all my life. In it I saw the atoll shining in the dawn, its palms swaying in the ocean breeze. Above the treetops stood a man-made thing—like a tree with no leaves, only taller. Suddenly it burst into a great ball of fire brighter than the sun and larger, spreading for a mile on either side of the island. A tall cloud rose up—red, purple, black, and white—and rained death on the sea. I heard a lament and a wail go up from the ocean. The cry was deafening. And I saw all the creatures of the sea pass one by one into that cloud. As they did, the light shone through their flesh and their flesh dissolved. Last I saw the shape of a man tall as the cloud pass into it. And the cloud burned away his flesh until only his bones remained. These glowed like fire, bright against the cloud, and vanished.

All of this happened in a few seconds. The vision passed, and I felt much older—very old. Until then I had never sung a song of my own, just the songs the pod sang. But a song came. And alone, by that bleached, moonlit waste, I sang to myself what I had seen, the Song of the Fireball:

> Tall over the trees stood the tree of man,
> From which grew a strange fruit, white and shining,
> A fireball fiercer than the falling sun,
> Brighter and broader than the burning island.
> It ate the trees and the coral under them
> And swallowed the creatures that swam in the current,
> Raining death in the dark on the blackest deep,
> Leaving a waste both wan and white,
> Nothing but fishbones where a fair folk finned it.
> I saw man's skeleton dissolve in the cloud
> Where he plucked a fruit of fire, deadly to fetch.

When I finished singing, I heard the echo of my song return, thin and ghostly, from the moon-washed cliffs of the dead reefs. The sense of a listening presence was strong, and I shivered and swam away from that blighted sea. Thoughtful, I returned to the pod and told no one what I had seen, nor sang to them the Song of the Fireball.

The waters grew gradually colder as we traveled south, and at night we slept in a tighter ring, the elders keeping watch. Once or twice we saw red and green lights skimming the horizon and heard the distant *thrug thrug* of an iron monster. Taking no chances, the whole pod would dive and change course, coming up only to breathe. A single ship might be a pirate whaler, complete with echo finders like our own. The most wicked of all whalers, they would, given the chance, devour a pod to the last calf.

One morning a bump on the horizon turned out to be not a ship but an iceberg. We swam by its majestic white shape, emerald at the edges and blue in the shadows. It was so large I felt a thrill of something like fear but more pleasant. I asked Hrūna about it, and he said the feeling was *awe*, and that it was one of the best feelings—when caused by the right object.

Soon a white line on the horizon revealed we had reached the Ice at the End of the World. As we drew closer, it loomed larger. Again I felt awe, and again it was a much better feeling than the one in the vision of the fireball, for I knew that the ice formed a wall which protected us whales. We heard the Singing of the Ice, the constant vibrations high and low the ice field made as it advanced to the sea and the giant icebergs broke, groaning and crashing into the water with shattering falls of loose ice. While the icebergs jostled and scraped together, seeking sea room, the song became a chorus rivaling in volume the song of a large pod. The eerie groanings, creakings, and wrenching screams blended together in a wild symphony that we whales joined as we approached, singing the Song of the Ice.

Later we swam under the icebergs, immersed in their music and in the emerald light from above that shifted as the ice shifted. It was an eerie but beautiful world. Under the ice shelf itself everything glowed a dim blue, and we didn't go in far past the edge, since there was no place to come up and breathe. Where the ice was thinnest, cracks of light shone through, bathing everything in cobalt or powder blue. All things floated in this strange void, and there was nothing to fix upon. There was no bottom, just a blue abyss with a ceiling graced by crystals that grew down in fantastic shapes. These shattered to a tinkling music when I swam through them.

Lewtë had told us of young whales losing their way and drowning under the ice shelf or becoming trapped when ice suddenly closed over the krill beds. But during the polar summer the ice was thawing, and water between the mountains of ice opened up into lagoons where a pod could rest safely on a summer's night.

From the tallest iceberg three of the largest birds I had ever seen—all snowy white—flew down with cries of welcome. They landed on the heads of Hrūna and Lewtë, who introduced me to a family of albatrosses: Ala, Ali, and their offspring, Ross. Their wingspread was the length of Hrūna's flipper, and they could hover on an updraft for hours, keeping a lazy lookout for approaching ships and warning the pod below. Ross flew over to my back. He asked if I could fly, since I was all white like an albatross. I said no, but I hoped he could swim. We both laughed at that, and he did three flips in the air. I tried to do the trick but fell on my head halfway through the second flip.

"Show-offs!" said Aleea and swam after her parents, who were headed for the krill beds.

I had long heard about the krill, but I couldn't believe my eyes when I first saw that ocean of pinkish orange shrimp, densely packed for miles and extending down deeper than I could dive. With one twitch of my tail I swam into that gorgeous sea salad, opening my mouth till it was full, then shut it and swallowed. I'll never forget that first taste of it. It brought tears to my eyes, and still does, when I've been away for half a year. I opened and swallowed again.

Aleea followed close behind me. Unfortunately, too close. About twenty yards into the krill I felt a sharp pain in my flukes and cried out.

"Excuse me," Aleea said, her mouth stuffed with krill. "I wasn't looking where I was biting." Except for herring and an occasional flounder, this was my first adult food. I spent whole days swimming in that wonderful sea, eating my weight in krill and, according to Hrūna and Lewtë, visibly growing each day. The grown-ups cut wide swaths into the heart of the bed that we calves used as paths in and out. The pod had had little food since the summer before and needed to replace the blubber that had shrunk over the winter.

Ross and I became good friends. The albatross perched on my head whenever I surfaced. Always hungry and feeling more sure of myself, each day I plunged into the krill farther from the pod. One afternoon just before I turned back, I heard sharp cries speeding toward me underwater and I breached. Ross was at the surface, flapping in a frenzy.

"Swim!" he cried. "Black fins. About fifteen of them moving toward you in a half circle."

"Sharks," I thought, starting toward the pod, and bid Ross fly for help. The whistles came louder even as I bent my flukes with all my might, regretting the ton of krill in my belly that slowed me down.

The shrill cries came on fast—much too fast—though I was swimming at top speed. Something black and white flashed by me and disappeared in the krill ahead. Then a black-and-white shape flashed on my other side. Confused, I shied left, then veered back on course toward the pod. The cries were all about me now. The krill suddenly vanished, and I saw swimming parallel to me, with all its teeth exposed, a Killer whale. My stomach dropped.

The Killer gave a sharp murderous cry, which was answered to my left. In terror I called out to Hrūna and Lewtë. No answer. The Killer whale on my right turned toward me, passing over my dorsal and whistling three times. He was answered by a half dozen cries close behind.

The two closed in, one on either side, rolling and eyeing me with hideous grins. The pack behind was gaining but I still swam as fast as I could, giving out the distress cry. At last I heard Hrūna's and Lewtë's faint response. As their cries grew louder, I thought the Killers pulled back ever so little. The two no longer crossed in front of me but pressed close behind as I swam terrified. They called back and forth a number of times in a language I did not understand. Then the larger moved alongside and opened his mouth. I shrieked, I guess, for he laughed and said with a thick accent, "Do not *ffeeyer*, leetle whale. I am Uton, your ffather's ffriend."

Before I could think of a reply, I saw Hrūna's hump speeding toward me (with a cyclone of feathers circling above it). Uton called out to him and Lewtë. In a moment I was between my parents, like the calf I had been a few months earlier. Both greeted the black-and-white Killer whale warmly. Uton, it turned out, was the one Hrūna had rescued with Lewtë from the lagoon years ago.

While they talked, Uton's whole pod pulled up, sleek black and white, with fiercely sharp teeth, but friendly enough and a little shy when introduced. Ross flew down and perched on my head, and they all laughed.

"Your *yong*ster here," Uton said, spouting a laugh, "he swim too *ffar* from the pod, *nyet*? I think he need *good* lesson, so we chase him home. *Yes?*" He laughed again, showing all his teeth, and the other Killer whales joined him.

I didn't think it was at all funny, but I laughed from sheer relief. Hrūna and Lewtë talked to the Killer whales for an hour, until, at a whistle from Uton, they turned as one and sped away into the depths of the krill.

Chapter Five

DESPITE the warning from Uton, I went off more frequently by myself or with Ross, traveling farther and farther from the pod. But we kept our wits about us. Also, Hrūna took me on a number of overnight trips, schooling me in celestial navigation and the ways of the sea, its flora and fauna, winds and tides, and manifold dangers. More than once he stressed that of all creatures man was the most unpredictable—one time our apparent friend and another, our deadly enemy.

One starry morning before dawn Hrūna nudged me awake and signaled for me to follow him silently into the darkness. I did so, swimming hard to keep up with him. After the gray mists climbed from the water, he paused long enough to tell me we were going to the cave of Hralekana, my namesake, a journey of two days. At the end of the second day, as the sun crawled like a red crab over the horizon, he told me to breathe deeply in preparation for my longest dive yet. I did so, and down we plunged into the Green, then the Blue, and finally into the Black Deep. Hrūna faded in the cold dark, and I followed him only by his voice. The pressure on my ears was intense. The surface above had vanished, and I was afraid. I would soon have given up without Hrūna's patient encouragement from below.

Dim phosphorous lights appeared, belonging to strange fish whose bodies were strings of light shaped in odd ways. We sank below them until I felt like a clam squeezed in its shell. At length in the heavy dark another light appeared. It was the entrance to a tunnel, the sides of which glowed with some sort of phosphorescent stone. We swam up it to an enormous sea cavern that dwarfed even Hrūna. There, hanging from the ceiling and rising from the floor, stalactites and stalagmites showed like dark teeth against the pale blue light. Otherwise, it was empty.

Hrūna stopped at the entrance and was still. At last, pausing every few words, he told me how Grandfather Hrunta had brought him here at my age to meet Hralekana, the Great White Whale, who had broken his profound silence to speak with them.

"He was giant," Hrūna said, "and his head seemed to fill the cavern. I believe his mouth was wider than I was long." He told how Hralekana had related the history of the whales from the beginning and their sad struggle with men. The history was grim and took hours to recount. Last, Hralekana had prophesied Hrūna's leadership of the pod and in mysterious ways foretold the struggle with the whalers at the Ice at the End of the World in which Hralekana himself died a hero's death.

"That struggle was the greatest test I've ever had to face," Hrūna said with a faraway look in his eye. "Before Hralekana rose to do battle, I thought I was the one fated to take on the whalers." He paused and turned his face to the wall. When he spoke again, his voice was thick.

"Since you are his namesake and all white like him, I know he would want me to bring you here at this age. He would have liked to meet you." He paused again. "He would want you to know this place and perhaps to spend time here. By means that we other whales did not understand, he was able to lie down here for months without breathing at the surface, singing his song of one note that sounded as if it emanated from the heart of the earth."

Hrūna turned to face me. "I have already shared with you much that he told me. No doubt he would have special words for you, but I cannot fathom what those would be. I have thought long about what to say to you in his stead, and it has come to me to tell you how the Constellation of the Leaping Whale, which shines over our heads in these waters, came to be. This is the best I can do."

Hrūna stared off into the wall.

"There was once a whale who fell in love with a star. From underwater, the star looked large, warm, and close, its rays spreading in all directions. Above the water, however, it shrank to a pinpoint of light, steady and far away. One night the Humpback rose during a great calm and found the image of the star reflected, along with dozens of others, on the mirrorlike surface.

"'Aha!' he thought to himself. 'Now I will catch the star on top of the water.' But no matter how fast he swam toward it, just so fast it fled from him. Exhausted by these attempts, it occurred to him to dive under the reflection and to swallow it from below. From under the water he saw it again, wavering and warm above him, and rose quickly

61

with his mouth around it. He swallowed the reflection and for a moment felt a strange joy till, looking up, he saw the star clear and cold, at an infinite distance above him.

"Frustrated, he began to leap after it, causing the other whales to laugh. At each leap he went higher, though never coming close, desiring ever more ardently to take it into himself. By this means he became a mighty leaper. To the other members of his pod he seemed to have lost his mind, and they waggled their flippers at his ridiculous attempts.

"After many nights he stopped, worn out, and in despair sank into the Black Deep. There in the darkness he fell asleep and was wakened by a brilliant light under him that he recognized as the Whale of Light. Slowly the huge Whale rose and lifted him like a calf toward the top. Faster and faster he rose. When he reached the top, he flew right on up into the air, higher and higher, the Whale of Light under him. They rose far above the ocean and above the earth, which shrank to a small glimmer below. In the dark abyss of space, the Whale of Light propelled him ever closer to the star. Soon he saw that the star was larger than the earth and felt foolish ever to have thought he could swallow it.

"There in the cold of space he began to feel warmth from the star. Soon it pulled him toward itself, and he disappeared into its vast light. That which he thought to swallow had swallowed him.

"Strangely enough, the others who saw him take that highest of all leaps did not see the Whale of Light under him propelling him upward. All they saw was one of their own kind leaping higher than any had ever leaped.

"He was never seen again in this world, but it is said that he swims in the endless ocean of that star, one with what he desired.

"What's more, the drops that flew from his tail as he leaped that greatest of all leaps marked his path across the heavens. Ever since, the whales have seen his shape among the stars, and the Tail Spray still flies from the bending flukes of the Leaping Whale."

Hrūna stopped and looked at me a long while. I said nothing, imagining the glowing walls of that cave to be the inside of the star.

"Let us go up," he finally said. "Your lungs must be close to bursting."

I did not answer right away, and then said softly, "Not especially." For ever since he had started the tale, I felt no need to exchange the air in my lungs. A strange calm had come over me. Hrūna looked at me so oddly I began to move toward the entrance. We swam up to the surface without a word, and there it did seem good, mighty good, to breathe the fresh air again and hear the wash of the waves and the high mewling cry of the gulls.

From that day on I spent much time alone, sometimes leaving the pod for days. Often I returned to the great sea cavern by myself and descended to its glowing depths. I spent hours there—staying under longer than I could anywhere else—dreaming of the whale who loved a star and pondering the meaning. Sometimes I'd catch myself singing a simple song over and over.

There it came to me that soon I would leave the pod.

With this in mind, over the next few months I spent more time with Hrūna and Lewtë and my friends—especially Aleea. Feeding on the krill had spurred our growth. We were both nearing half our adult size, and somehow that made us shy with each other. Gone was the easy frolic of the lagoon, but we often spent hours swimming side by side, saying nothing.

Sometimes Aleea wouldn't let me near but swam lazily off by herself to some lonely space among the ice mountains where she listened to the wild singing of the ice. At such times I thought of the solitary star she wore on her forehead and spoke her full name, Alaleea, over and over to myself.

Once in the moonlight I found her alone, with Ross perched silently above her on the tip of an iceberg. That sight gave me an uncanny feeling of beauty and solitude I have never forgotten. It reminded me of an ancestor's song about an albatross from the days of wooden ships:

> In mist or cloud, on mast or shroud,
> It perched, for vespers nine,
> While all the night, through fog-smoke white,
> Glimmered the white Moonshine.

At long last, the cows heavy with calves to be born, the pod left the krill and the ice and returned to the warm islands of our birth. We yearlings stayed at a distance from the adults and the new calves when they were born and, hungry all the time, went far in search of herring, capelin, and other small fish.

One night it came to me that I must now depart on my Lonely Cruise around the world to gain knowledge of that world and to seek out who I am. In the morning I told Hrūna, Lewtë, and Aleea, and at first light the following day, after many good-byes, I swam due east into the golden scallop of the rising sun. A mile out from the pod I took three leaps and watched my parents and Aleea breach in unison, their flippers touched pink by the early sun. We sang to each other for many hours as I traveled, before their voices faded and I was truly alone.

Only then did I feel my stomach go hollow, but slowly a sense of exhilaration filled me. The sun was a white blaze, and stretching before me lay a long corridor of sea, green and golden in its light. I leaped three times for sheer joy and spouted a series of rainbow rings while singing the Song of the Open Sea:

> O, the sea lies all before me now,
> Where to wander at my own sweet will
> Like the gull who swoops and glitters in the light
> And circles the spindrift-tossing wave. . . .

A school of flying fish joined me for the rest of that day, a living rainbow of color arching over my back, now and then falling on me and flipping, with the high shrieks of fish, back into the sea.

Weeks passed as I swam east and south, chatting with the occasional gull or tern that rested on my back or picked sea lice from between my barnacles. I swam into heavy seas, where the sun grew hazy, the waves gray and restless in their swell, and gales drove the stinging spray straight across the water. I was nearing the first great obstacle about which Hrūna had warned me—the flukes or tail end of one of the giant land masses that sprawl across the ocean, reaching nearly to the Ice at the End of the World. At this cape the waters ran rough and freezing, filled with treacherous whirlpools and currents that could dash a whale upon a rock or reef. Many were the wrecks of ship-monsters strewn along that rocky cape, broken into pieces by wind and tide.

I stayed as close to the surface as I dared while not exposing myself to the wild waves. The sky grew dark at noon, and Ohobo stalked in fury from the west, his harpoon lighting that seascape an eerie green and shining from high, bare mountains that lined the shore. Once I was swept sideways by a current that tugged me toward a shallow basin opening in the waves, a whirlpool that would suck me down and smash me against rocks on the bottom. I turned and pulled away from it with all my strength.

A long dark night passed before the storm subsided, but I headed steadily east. When the sky grayed, I had left behind the worst of that cape, though the waves were still mountain-high.

Swimming along underwater, I heard two faint explosions. Surfacing, I saw green and red fires hanging in the air toward the coast over the largest iron monster I'd ever seen. Its hull was the length of twenty Humpbacks, and at one end rose a small white mountain with eyes like those on the broken ships by the lagoon. It was obviously in trouble. One end tilted out of the water, exposing a red stripe along the bottom. Tiny, split-fluked creatures were climbing over its side into little boats the sea slammed against the iron beast. Both ends quivered, and the middle was twisting and bending, making a groaning noise. It was caught on a reef.

I dove and swam toward the ship, and the surface suddenly darkened. Cautiously I surfaced and felt something sticky cover my blowhole. It stung. With difficulty, I breathed through it. It smelled awful, and my lungs burned. I lobtailed and sped back to clear water. My lungs on fire, I breached and saw a black fluid snaking over the sea toward me and spreading wide around the ship.

Oil. The dolphins had told us about this black grease men carried in iron monsters three times the length of a large whaling ship. If the oil ships broke up on rocks or sank, this poison spread for miles on top, suffocating the fish below and the birds that landed in it, killing the plants on the bottom and the otters, seals, and dolphins coated by it. Oil was not good to eat, and no one knew why men carried it in the bellies of their ships. Some thought the iron monsters fed on it.

Just then I heard the wail of gulls in distress. Three black oily creatures flopped at the edge of the oil spill, trying to fight their way out of the slimy mess. Heavy with it, they could not fly. And the slick spread rapidly around and beyond them. I had no choice but to help. I hated the burning taste the oil gave to the water, even the parts it had not yet covered, but I called out to the gulls to climb on my back and I swam right into the disgusting stuff. Somehow they managed to flop and scramble onto my head, and I carried them several miles upwind where the oil would not follow. More than once the gulls, too weak to talk, slid off my head, and I circled back for them in that rough sea.

Finally, I found a cove deep enough to enter, and the three flopped off to a stone beach where they lay still from exhaustion. Sadly I left them, thinking of Ross and his family and what oil would do to the albatrosses. When I came back to the spill, it was miles wide, and I had to swim far around it. Greasy black clouds of smoke mounted from flames near the ship. Men had set the sea on fire—or rather, the oil that floated on top. I heard a high whine and quickly dove as over me passed the largest bird I'd ever seen, with wings that stuck out stiff and unmoving. It made a constant whine and swam low over the waves, silver and shiny. From its tail it sprayed white stuff over the oil. Other birds with revolving wings, which I recognized as thunderwings from Hrūna's description, hovered over the ship, their shapes black against the orange flames. One flew near me, and I slipped under again, looking up at it through the water. A human creature hung from it by a rope.

There was a small splash above me, and I saw the creature wriggling in the water. From its movements, I was sure it was drowning. I rose to get a close look at it. It screamed and thrashed the water, attempting to get away, but then choked and slipped toward the bottom. I dove and lifted it above the water. It lay still across my back. I was fearful as the thunderwing returned, but I held myself steady. A second creature was hanging by the rope. The thunderwing hovered over me, and the second reached down and seized the first. Slowly it climbed the rope with the other, and the two disappeared into the thunderwing's belly. The bird sped away, and I swam deep and fast away from there.

Though the storm had waned, the waters remained rough and choppy. Part of me was eager to leave the cape behind, but another part wanted to stay in the neighborhood of the wreck. As the wind calmed, I began to pick up more sounds from the direction of the disaster. I heard the high, thin cries of fish sensing a change in the water passing through their gills. Worse, I heard the helpless cries of hundreds of gulls and other seabirds trapped in the heavy slick. Most pitiful of all were the cries of sea otters and seals fatally coated by the tarry mess. The oil ruined the insulating power of their fur and they died of the cold. Before that happened, they often rubbed themselves bloody trying to clean it off.

Steeling myself to the burning taste, I swam under the oil toward these cries and brought many an otter and seal out to clean water and left it on a rocky beach. In order to carry the victim in my mouth, I had to take in some of the oil. This I spat out later, but the bad taste remained with me for days. Weeks later I occasionally spat out a tarry chunk of it caught between plates of baleen. Fortunately, I was able to hold a pocket of air in my mouth for the victim, or it would never have survived the trip out. Afterwards it was often too weak to thank me, and I wondered if the oil would ever come off its fur.

Meanwhile the oil spread like the shadow of death over the ocean, covering many miles. The whole region grew more silent. More ships arrived. It looked as if they were trying to take the oil back inside them or spraying something to dissolve it, but their efforts were no match for the enormous slick, which spread with a will of its own. I did see a pod of men along the shore pick up oil-covered otters and gulls and put them into large shells. Later the gulls came out much whiter, walking about. One or two even flew away. How strange, I thought, this human creature was, one moment destroying thousands, the next rescuing a few. As Hrūna was fond of saying, who could fathom man?

After three days the cries of trapped victims grew faint and then disappeared altogether. To a Humpback's ears the ocean is alive with sound, from the hiss a clam makes when it squirts water, to the mightiest roar of an angry bull whale. That whole shore was usually a teeming nursery for dozens of kinds of birds, otters, and seals—not to mention plankton, shrimp, and other shellfish. Now an ominous silence came from it that spoke louder than any cry of the dying. I guessed that if I passed that shore again, I would find it bone-empty and silent as the sea around the vanished atoll.

Chapter Six

W EAK from hunger and the dizzying effect of the oil, I swam on to fresher waters. Later by some shoals I found an abundance of herring and fed for several days. On one shoal I met a solitary Blue whale, his belly sulfur-colored like a sunset after a storm. He was a yearling like myself and named Bala. He expressed surprise at my color, but even more that I was a Humpback, since I was as long as he. (The Blues are usually the largest of all whales.) He said he'd parted from his mother a number of days earlier. He had never seen his father, nor any Blue except his mother. She told him there were so few Blue whales left, he might well be the last one born. He was eager for company, and the two of us decided to swim to warmer waters together.

Bala was not really a singer—his songs were short and contained obvious kinds of meaning—but he was an excellent acrobat. It was impressive to watch his huge golden belly roll in and out of the water, reflecting sunlight as he spun, creating a small tidal wave. We played for hours sometimes, rocking ourselves silly on each other's waves.

At last we reached islands in warm water. There we found several pods of Humpbacks passing the winter. They often encountered men in small boats, they told us, and at times these swam in the water with them. Fascinated, I asked what humans looked like swimming, and the whole pod laughed.

One answered, "Somewhat like a lobster, only with the head where the tail should be and its flukes waggling behind like two claws." The swimming humans had not hurt the whales, and so fragile were they, the Humpbacks had to be careful not to brush them with flipper or fluke. Those in the small boats, though noisy, also seemed harmless enough.

Still hungry, and anxious to explore the world, Bala and I cruised through the tropical waters toward the opposite Pole. The water again grew colder and more wild. We found many shoals filled with herring. Because each of us was so large, the two of us agreed to feed on separate shoals, and we gradually lost track of each other.

One day I heard a bellow that sounded like Bala's, and I left the shoal to look for him in deep waters. I saw something flash far below me and gathered from the grunts and cries that a life-and-death struggle was going on in the Black Deep. As I descended, I heard a wild trumpeting and saw the dim shadow of a huge head move toward the surface, dragging something gray behind it. Rising, I was in time to witness the triumphal spout of a large square head belonging to a Sperm whale. His small lower jaw, filled with large teeth, was closing on the last remnants of a squid's tentacles. The Sperm whale's broad back was a network of round scars and bleeding cuts. He was crusted with barnacles.

"Be well!" I hailed him.

"Blast and avast!" the Sperm whale answered. "Are you whale or ghost?" Still chewing the last of the squid, he swam over and eyed me flipper to fluke. "Are you a Humpback or a bleached-out Blue?"

74

"A Humpback," I said, piqued by his bluff manner. "Who is so rude as to ask?"

"Spygga the Sperm whale," he replied, spitting out the last of a tentacle.

"I've had a taste of what you Sperm whales chew on, and I can't blame you for spitting it out," I observed.

His wrinkled eyelid opened wide. "Well, have you now? Since when do you weed strainers go in for real fish?"

I told him of the battle with the giant squid, and I could see, off-flipper and casual as he pretended to be, that he was impressed.

"Well, blow me down!" he finally conceded. "You'll make a shrimp gulper of me yet, though you'll never make me into one of your groaners and whoopers. I saves me breath for better things!" He ducked and spouted again. I could tell he meant no harm by his rough manner, and this last remark, I learned later, was as close to a compliment as the bluff old warrior gave.

I told him then of the oil spill and he frowned, the hide around his eye crinkling severely.

"Aye, but what will the split-flippers think of next? My people have been skewered and all but swallowed out of the sea. You'll find men even more cruel in this ocean than in yours. They kill us sometimes for no reason and in devilishly clever ways."

Spygga proceeded to tell me the history of the Sperm whales in that part of the ocean.

"For years they hunted us with monsters made of trees to which they tied large white clouds that were driven along

75

by the wind. Then, in my great-granddaddy's day, they came with faster ships, made of iron, that growled and smoked and spat fire. These new ships could spit iron into us, where it exploded, crippling us without a struggle. They inflated us with air so that we died in agony floating on the surface. Last, the giant ships swallowed us and pulled us apart." He struck the water angrily with his flukes.

"You know about this from your ocean, but there are things that happened here you may not have heard of. Crueller than the harpooners were those who trapped the Sei whales and the Fins in fjords and coves with explosions and nets, who then stuck long dirty knives in them so they would die slowly of disease.

"But I'll tell you a stranger thing. In Grandfather's day humans stopped hunting us for a few years and hunted each other. They came out in many ships to spit fire that exploded inside other ships as harpoons did in us. The ships burned and sank to the bottom, and the men in them drowned. The sea was filled with their dead. Strangest of all was the iron whale the humans made that swam under the surface like us, and like us went to the surface to breathe. This iron whale, though it had no eyes, also like us knew where to go underwater by listening to echoes. We heard men moving about inside. Often an iron whale floated in one place, waiting for the large ship-monsters. When one passed, it spat long iron fish from its mouth. These swam very fast and straight and with fire knocked a hole in the ship's bottom, and it sank. Sometimes the iron whale spat these things at night in rough seas, and scores of ships burned and sank to the bottom. When it had done this, other ships came—fast, narrow ones—and dropped large shells that exploded underwater. The explosions were deafening. If a whale was nearby, the explosion cracked his head and he died. Sometimes the explosions cracked open one of the iron whales, and it sank to the bottom, letting out some of the oily stuff.

"Though we whales increased in numbers during these years, we sometimes came to a sad end. Iron birds flew over the ocean to drop explosive eggs on the iron whales. Sometimes they dropped the eggs on real whales instead. This happened to my poor Great Uncle Spergo and to my cousin Spynna. Spynna was not killed, but she went crazy from the explosion and swam up on shore and suffocated."

He paused, and a film of tears moved over his eyes.

"Men must have lost what little wit they had, because the whales they killed this way sank to the bottom. They could not possibly eat them. And why would humans kill each other, for surely they do not, like sharks, feed on one another?"

He paused for a long while, staring vacantly.

"At last, the battles between men ceased, and they started hunting us again. Iron whales continued to swim in our waters, though they no longer hunted the ships. But now they have grown even larger, until they are many times the size of the largest whale. We still hear men move around inside of them and we hear their echo finders. They swim very quietly now and lie still, waiting for another iron whale to pass, which they then stalk at a distance. Sometimes they pursue a real whale instead, until they lose interest and turn away.

"In recent years we have seen another terrible thing. Sometimes the iron whales are accompanied by dolphins swimming alongside. These dolphins do not answer when we speak and have a strange look in their eyes. Often metal things are fastened to their heads. It's as if their brains have been taken away and they are no longer free to be themselves. They follow the iron whale's every move and communicate with the men inside. Since they do not speak to us, we cannot learn why they go with the humans.

"Though the iron whales do not spit iron fish at each other any longer, we know they have death inside them. We sense death in the water wherever they are. There is a burning in them that is not good; we feel it come from them. We call it the Invisible Burning. Sometimes iron monsters come and drop large shells full of this Burning into a deep canyon. We feel the Invisible Burning through the shells and stay far away from that place.

"So the humans still harm us, though my great-grandfather helped save their lives many years ago when the largest iron monster of all challenged the iceberg and lost."

Appalled by all he had told me, I was nevertheless intrigued by this last remark. I had never heard of an iron monster challenging one of the great ice-mountains. At the End of the World the whalers stayed far away from the ice. "What do you mean, 'challenged the iceberg'?" I asked.

"My great-grandfather, Spyrta, was a yearling and swimming alone by himself north toward the Pole when the year

78

was warming, looking for the kraken—the giant squid. In those days the iron monsters were, as a rule, smaller than now. There were none of the large ships that swallow whales and certainly none of the giant ones swollen with oil in their gut.

"Spyrta was swimming north, longing for the cold waters and the mountains of ice. You can well imagine his excitement when he saw a small ice floe or two float by. He sent out his cry regularly, listening intently for an echo from any large object that might be an iceberg. Faintly, due north of him, he picked up the echo from one larger than he had ever seen. He felt a strange thrill move through him as it drifted toward him.

"You know the feeling of which I speak, Hralekana, for you have been among the ice. It is the feeling of fear and pleasure mixed. Spyrta eagerly swam on toward the iceberg, crying out and stretching to hear every sound in the Deep. It was then he picked up a whisper of something large moving from the east, hundreds of miles away. At first, he thought it was another iceberg, but it was not floating in the right direction to be one. And it was coming on too fast. Large as an iceberg, yet not one, it puzzled him, until at last he heard the dim churning of engines and the *thrug thrug* of three giant screws. It was a ship-monster. But what a ship— three to four times larger than those he was used to seeing! In those days there were fewer ship sounds in the sea, and these were clear and unmixed. From the wash of small sounds that accompanied the louder ones, he could tell there were many humans aboard, as many as krill in a pouch.

"Immediately he wanted to see the ship as well, and for a minute or two he was torn. Then a wild joy filled him as he realized that the two monsters, if they kept on course, were likely to pass close to one another.

"He swam north as fast as he could and late in the afternoon caught sight of the giant iceberg. There was the mountain—white, emerald, blue, pink, depending on the light—towering to the heavens while showers of ice crashed down its sides and plumes of mist rose from the water. It gleamed and flashed as it slowly turned. His ears told him that under the water lay a hulk of ice eight times larger than the mountain looming before him. That dark green and blue bulk, which ordinarily sang a wild and harsh music as it ground against other ice, now moved absolutely silent through the depths like some sleeping monster dreaming toward its prey.

"His tongue stuck in his throat at the sight. Cautiously, he circled the iceberg underwater. It was a long time before he dared approach very close. But he stayed with that ice mountain as it drifted lazily but steadily south, while the gulls that made it their floating home shrieked and landed on his back when he rose to breathe. All this time he heard the screws of the great ship, still scores of miles distant, grow louder, and he knew it would pass nearby in the middle of the night.

"That evening the sun sank, a blood-red eye in the west. Seen against it, the iceberg loomed, a jagged black shape. But from the west he saw the luminous ice, a polar pink at first, darken to fiery red and then purple as the last light sank and a star or two steered across open reaches of sky. Last, mists from the surface writhed and danced around the iceberg, now a ghostly white against black water.

"He slept for a while by the side of the iceberg and was wakened at midnight by the *thrug thrug* of the screws accompanied by strains of music and other sounds: the rattle of machinery, the clang of iron on iron, the thousand soft scuffles and thuds of humans aboard the iron monster. To the east the sky glowed faintly, and then, above the horizon rose a light—several lights—and a white tip like the top of an iceberg. While he watched, this grew into the superstructure of an iron monster, white and gleaming with a thousand eyes. As it rose higher, he cried out where he lay in the iceberg's shadow, for he could see its whole length and the ship was longer than a dozen Blues or more. Four such ships put head to flukes would equal a mile. Four huge iron logs leaned into the air from its top and belched black smoke and sparks swirling like stars. It was coming on as fast as a whale in fear could swim, and it would pass very close indeed.

"The strains of music floated clearly through the air, and he said that he never forgot them, nor could he put them out of his head. The ship was only several miles away, and high wings of water glowed like phosphorus where the nose of the ship cut through it. He marveled at the giant ship until, instinctively, a slow horror spread through him from flipper to fluke: unless the ship changed direction, it would meet the iceberg head on.

"Paralyzed, he stared from the shadow of the iceberg

while the ship came straight on, unwavering. What kind of creature was this ship, to challenge a mountain of ice? The thought occurred to him that men might be out to destroy the iceberg, to hunt it the way they hunted whales. Would the sharp nose of the ship cut right through it? But that was impossible, for the iceberg was too large—even larger underwater.

"Fascinated, he forced himself to swim away from the iceberg, crossing the line of the approaching ship with a shudder. Several hundred yards south he turned to watch. Still the ship did not change course and came on at great speed, its whole top lit like day itself, the haunting music reeling over the air above the deep *thrug thrug* of the screws. He could see tiny black shadows crawling in twos or threes along the decks.

"It was a strange sight, and he felt very odd. He'd known since early that day that these two giants were headed toward each other—as if each had come hundreds of miles across the sea to meet the other. Was it a battle of nerves, like that of two bull males trying to face each other down when both loved the same cow? No, it was more than that. He held his breath.

"He saw a figure or two scurry about the nose of the ship. Suddenly it changed direction. The ship-monster was going to go right by the iceberg—close—but it did not intend to hit it. There was a thrashing and whining as the screws went into reverse.

"The lights blazed as closer and closer the two giants drew until, in the last few seconds, the lights from the

82

ship's white top eerily lit the white ice. The ship was going to make it—just.

"But then a heart-wrenching tearing and screaming of steel vibrated through the water, and the ship visibly shuddered and faltered. It had struck the iceberg along its side underwater. The huge berg groaned, twisted, and drifted away. The *thrug thrug* ceased as the engines stopped dead in the water. The smoke dwindled and vanished.

"The haunting music stopped—and then started up again.

"Over the next hour Spyrta saw the strangest sight yet. Thousands of the tiny black figures crawled out of the top. Their voices were high and short and washed over him like a distant surf. Alien as their cries were, he felt their distress and fear. Bright fires flew high into the air and hovered there for seconds. He knew from the sound of metal tearing that the monster had torn open its iron belly. Gradually, while he watched, the nose of the ship sank lower into the sea. The crowd of shadows on board lowered tiny boats into the water, which calm, gleamed with the lights of the ship and a few stars. Many humans were in these boats. Others dropped from the decks into the water and were picked up. Some of the boats were full, others partly empty. Still more remained hanging on the side of the ship. The music played on.

"The ship's nose sank lower and lower, but the lights still burned. Soon all the boats pulled away from the sides, though many humans were still on board. Last, with a grandeur that shook through Spyrta, the ship rose up on its bow and hung there a moment, lights shining. Spyrta saw hundreds of the tiny creatures still clinging to its top and heard cries of panic and fear, along with the voices of others singing. Then with a majestic and deadly ease it slid beneath the waves while a great mournful shout rose from the people in the boats. A wave passed over the ocean with a sigh. The night was dark again, except for the ghostly white of the iceberg floating a mile to the south and a handful of stars, whose reflection rose and fell once on the spreading ripple.

"He heard many voices calling out from the boats and the cries of those helpless in the water who had jumped from the ship at the last moment. Spyrta swam around the boats to where the ship had been and, coming up from under, pushed three struggling survivors to the side of a boat without showing himself. He found a dozen more by their cries and repeated the rescue. He often wondered what the half-frozen drowning made of the force that pushed them toward the boats—if they were even aware of it in their state of shock. He was sure he had not been seen. For with the passing of the ship of lights, the night was dark except for the luminous shadow floating south."

Spygga paused, and we lay there side by side for a long while. I was mesmerized by this tale of a ship of lights that challenged an iceberg and sank over a mile into the Black Deep. And I secretly wished to see the ship. I wondered long about the music that continued playing to the end and about those who went singing into the Deep.

Chapter Seven

T HE night was black by the time Spygga finished, and we slept there on the shoals, the stars swimming over us like a million herring. In the morning I asked Spygga the question that had been troubling me. "Did anyone follow the ship into the Deep to see what became of it?"

He looked at me a long time before answering. "Yes, my great-grandfather marked the spot by the stars. Later he returned and dove, and so has each generation of our family. I went down to it—once."

"Would you go again?"

"It is a very deep dive, dangerously deep." Spygga was not eager to make the dive a second time, but at long last I convinced him to lead me on it. After a journey of several days we reached the waters of the sinking. That night Spygga located the spot by the stars, and at dawn we started down. Green, then blue, then black, the water was cold and heavy. The pressure closed in and made me feel like a whelk squeezed far back into its shell. We said little to each other and kept in touch by echo. After several hours the echo told us the ocean floor was near.

At the bottom we found each other in the darkness and swam over a small ridge. There a weird sight met our eyes. In long strings, in squares and triangles, in star shapes and fantastic loops, swam the electric fish of the Deep, their transparent flesh radiant with bluish white light. Hundreds, perhaps thousands, of them clustered there, and in the faint radiance we saw the outline of a great ship, broken into two parts, but nevertheless resting upright and majestic on the bottom. It loomed there, its superstructure intact, staring at us with a thousand dark eyes through the dim light. Though rusted and tarnished, the ship was remarkably free of weeds at this depth. In and out of windows and through the rip in her belly wove the luminous fish like the ghosts of lights with which she challenged the night so long ago.

The pressure was great, the cold intense, and we did not speak, saving our strength. We swam to the high rusted side of the ship and rose level with the mountain of eyes on top. We peered through the largest of these into a vast space filled with the weaving lights of electric fish. They circled around each other, wavering as they advanced and retreated in rhythm, as if to some unheard music that wound from the belly of that splendid ship.

Caught up in the music, I had another Seeing. Suddenly the dark space was brightly lit, and I saw many pairs of humans moving about to music, face to face, one dark as a seal and the other in colors as bright or delicate as an anemone's. Around the necks and on the flippers of the bright ones flashed pebbles like those Aleea and I found in the wooden ship. The music was sweet, yearning high and low. I thought sadly that the pairs might be mates, and this circling together was their courting.

The vision faded as quickly as it came. Stare as I might, all I saw now were the slowly circling fish. Gone were the lights, gone the music of that night, and gone the fair folk who by the thousands sailed blithely to meet the great, imperturbable iceberg. Now like some reef of the southern seas the ship lay, broken in two, a home for ghostly fish who lit an endless night and never saw the day.

Spygga signalled it was time to leave. We rose to the surface slowly to avoid the sickness that comes from the change in the water's weight. We didn't speak much about what we'd seen, and I knew now why he had gone there only once before.

After returning to the shoals, Spygga and I parted, and I cruised west looking for better fishing grounds. These I shared not only with Sei and Fin whales but with men in small ships who pulled in fish by the hundreds in long nets. Feeding in these waters, I had to be careful not to become tangled in the mile-long nets, which they often let drift for days. I found a dolphin miserably circling inside one and pressed it down so that he could swim out. He told me that hundreds of his kind were not so lucky. Caught in these nets, they starved or were killed. Birds who landed on the nets were pulled under and drowned.

The fishermen did not bother me, though they often sailed close and shouted to each other when they saw me. There were many small islands in those waters and rocks breaking just above the surface, so at a distance I blended in with these. As a calf I'd heard a story of a sleeping whale men mistook for an island. They beached their boat on his back, but he didn't wake until they started a fire to cook their fish. With a roar he lobtailed, scattering the fishermen and their fire to the waves. Mothers told their calves this tale to warn them to stay alert. But I fished close to the men for days without incident, until a fog arose and the boats left for shore.

Having had my fill of herring for a while, I swam again to deeper waters to explore them. I cruised through the green depths almost half a day before picking up by echo what I first thought was a Blue whale. I soon sensed it was far larger than a whale. It was moving swiftly toward me and might be an iron monster, but it did not make the usual sounds of ships. The only noise it made was a whisper like the faintest breathing from a blowhole. Even more strange, it was a hundred fathoms under the surface.

Curiosity got the better of me, and I plunged down to take a look at it. At first I couldn't see anything in the Blue Deep. Then up from the Black Deep a long shadow rose, and my heart jumped. I hung there, above and to one side, as the dark shape slid past. It was swollen and elongated like a whale, but as long as a large ship. It had no eyes, but it did have stubby flukes and fins. From its back rose a tall fin like a Killer whale's. I could tell from the echo that its skin was iron, and from inside it came the muffled voices of men. It was pushed by two giant screws, slow and silent.

My uneasiness increased as the iron whale passed, but not from fear of its size nor the presence of men. Something inside it—I couldn't say what—made me feel weak. There was an evil thing there, a great power for destruction. The feeling reminded me of the Waste Sea and the vision of the fireball. I recalled Spygga's strange talk of the Invisible Burning.

With a whisper it made a quarter turn and sank into the Black Deep. I hovered there recalling all that Spygga had said about the iron whales. It was long out of hearing when I picked up the sound again, coming from the same direction as before. Soon a second iron whale emerged from the Black Deep—this one a slightly different shape. It came just as quietly and turned where the first one had. I wondered why it was following the other. Were they of the same pod? Or was it an enemy, hunting the other?

Foolishly, considering these uneasy thoughts, I followed it. It zigzagged in a circle to the right, but I kept on its track. After a while it sank deeper than I cared to go, so I veered off and continued eastward. I'd almost forgotten it when an echo returned, telling me the iron whale was now following *me*. Alarmed, I changed course and depth several times trying to shake it off but to no avail. Soon I heard a small explosion and sensed a thin object speeding toward me. It was coming faster than I could swim, and immediately I turned a full quarter and sank into the Blue Deep, recalling the steel fish Spygga had warned me about. I swam a few flipper lengths and turned again onto still another course.

My ears told me the steel fish was turning in a wide circle searching for me. I was now swimming directly back toward the iron whale. I may have been foolhardy, but I thought if it spat any more steel fish, I could dodge them head-on more easily than run from them. Behind, the first steel fish had found my scent and was closing in rapidly.

Desperate, I swam straight toward the iron whale. In a minute its black shadow appeared, swelling in the dim light. Meanwhile, the steel fish behind me was closing at twice my speed. I had only a few seconds to act. The iron whale's nose loomed in front of me. With my last strength I bent my flukes and dove beneath the hull of the iron whale. For a moment I was caught in a current and sucked toward the turning screws. Above me I heard a repeated harsh sound and the trampling of feet. Even as I pulled free, wheels turned, levers clanged, and the iron whale turned and plunged deeper.

Glancing up, I saw a thin silver object spurt above the iron whale, narrowly missing its high fin. A few yards farther on, it wavered back and forth, as if seeking the scent of its prey. It started slowly forward again, then stopped, as the jet of water from its tail vanished, and sank lazily into the depths. A moment later a distant explosion shook the ocean floor.

I went cold with fear when I thought how close the killer steel fish had come to me. Whistles, clangs, and buzzes sounded in the belly of the iron whale, and it reversed direction, rising toward the surface. A human voice inside it was loud with fear. The steel fish had almost bitten the iron whale that spat it. Without meaning to, I had led the fish back upon the iron whale and by so doing saved my life.

I plunged into the Black Deep and was followed no more. But I wondered, had the second iron whale mistaken me for the one it was following? Yet I was only a fraction of its size. Also, Spygga had said the iron whales did not fire at one another now. Was it trying to harpoon me with the steel fish? Whatever, the iron whales were not to be trusted, unlike the fishing boats I fed quietly among.

After my pulse slowed, I rose and swam far to the west, eventually coming to craggy islands, covered with birds, and a wild rocky coast.

That was the first I ever spent much time near a coast. I was curious about the fishers who returned to it every few days. Here and there their boats pulled into a cove, loaded with fish, and hoisted them by the netful onto the land. At night under cover of darkness I followed one in. Their dwellings looked like large white reefs or rocks scattered about, with caves the men walked into on their flukes. On land humans were agile. Many large eyes in these rocks shone bright, like those on iron monsters. But I could not linger long, because of the bitter taste of the water. It smacked of oil, rotten fish, and other decaying things.

Along that rocky coast was an abundance of fish, including my favorite, herring—often in places where fishing boats could not go because of rocks and shoals. There was one special cove that herring crowded into when the tide was high. I'd follow after, my mouth open, and scoop them up by the ton.

I stayed near this cove for several days. A few Finners and Seis passed by, leaving the fish to me. When full, I basked in the summer sun, thinking back on the pod. I wondered how many of the other yearlings had now left on the Lonely Cruise. Yet I was not homesick. I stared at the bald gray mountains, wreathed with clouds, and dreamed of moving past them onto land. I wondered more than ever what it was like to be human and to cross that land walking upright on flukes.

One night in a dream I heard the song of our pod. I woke in the darkness and listened hard but heard nothing. I went back to sleep, and the next morning woke restless, wishing for company. Later, while feeding, I heard a few distant notes of a Humpback. In my eagerness, I spat out a mouthful of fish and sang a greeting to whoever it was. In a few moments a faint greeting returned. I leaped clear out of the water, for I would know that voice anywhere. I answered and swam as fast as I could out to sea. Within half a morning a familiar spout rose on the horizon. I leaped again and smacked the surface three times. In response rose the form dearest to me in all the ocean.

In a few minutes Aleea and I were nose to nose, her white star shining before me, then flipper to flipper. We rolled and hugged, nudged and butted all the way back to the coast, while she told me her story. She had left on her Lonely Cruise not long after I did. Heading east, she passed the stormy cape and steered far south to avoid the oil spill, which had spread wide and stank of death. A bedraggled sea otter told her a white Humpback had passed that way and saved his life. When she turned north again, a school of dolphins repeated the news. Finally, she had the good luck to run into a pod of Sperm whales, including Spygga. He pointed her toward the herring grounds.

That afternoon I showed her my favorite cove where the herring ran. As the tide rose, herring streamed into it, drawn by its wealth of plankton, and we had a feast. We swam in eagerly after them, so thick we hardly needed to bubble-net. While we stuffed ourselves, I admired the new length and beauty of Aleea, her white streak extending from her flippers along both sides. She was half again her former length, and she declared I must already be as large as Hrūna.

The cove was a wild and beautiful place at the foot of a mountain. Gulls lined the rocky shore, waiting to swoop upon our leavings. On our third run up it, most of the herring had disappeared. We couldn't understand this since a moment before they had flashed in front of us, thick as ever. It was Aleea who discovered where they'd gone. Where the water grew shallow over a pebble bottom lay the entrance to a lagoon, or large sea pond. The herring had all swum into it to feed upon its rich plankton and minnows.

Scraping our bellies, we were able to follow them through the narrow inlet to the pond, wide and deep and still, and feast to our heart's content. Too soon for me, Aleea called that the tide was going out and we must leave. There was a knot of herring at one end, and I called back to her to go ahead, that I would come soon.

"*Now!*" she cried. "We must go now." I heard her scrape the pebbles at the narrow neck of the pond. Torn, I saw the herring cluster and lunged toward them. In a moment I had swallowed the mouthful and turned to swim the length of the pond. Aleea was already out in the cove calling to me in a worried voice.

"I'm right here," I said as, scraping my belly on the pebbles, I crunched to a full halt. Backing up, I tried once again, but the water fell even lower as the tide slipped out with a few lucky herring. I charged the pebbles once more with all my strength, my head half out of water. Stuck, I thrashed my flippers against the rocks, cutting them, but could not budge more than half my length. The water was dangerously low and, feeling crushed by my own weight out of water, with one last push of my flippers I thrust myself back into the pond.

I tried at two other points, but both were shallower than the first. Reluctantly, I called to Aleea, "I'm trapped. I'll have to wait for the next flood tide." I felt chagrin at my foolish neglect of her warning.

"Don't worry," she said. "I'll wait here," and spouted to show me where she was.

The tide wouldn't be up until evening and the herring were mostly gone from the pool, except for a few stragglers flashing among the rocks. I decided to rest on the bottom, where I was less likely to be seen. Neither of us had the slightest inkling of what lay ahead before the next high tide.

Chapter Eight

I woke to find a small boat floating above me, long sticks swinging out of it, pushing it along. Carefully I rose just under the surface where the image broke and wavered on the water. Only one human was in the boat, and he not full-grown, a yearling. I surfaced half a flipper away.

"Be well!" I sang out our traditional greeting. The creature stared, dropping the sticks, before replying with a faint sound. I eased alongside the fragile boat. Small as he was, the human reached out a short white flipper and stroked my side. Surprised by this, I whistled and clicked with pleasure like a calf, bobbing under and back up.

The human youth hesitated, looking as if he were thinking. I whistled and slapped my tail three times to encourage him. Then he did a strange thing. He peeled off what looked like his skin and jumped into the water alongside me, flailing and making all kinds of strange noises.

He was about the size of a sea lion, but white and scrawny, with split flukes. He had a band of blue skin around his middle. He ran his flipper along my side up to my flipper. I held mine out, hoping he would grasp it. He didn't, so I moved forward and stuck it out again, trusting he would get the idea. At last he did, grasping it—not with his teeth, which were too weak, but with his own flippers, divided at the end like a sea otter's. In fact, this creature looked a bit like a sea otter, if you can imagine one with no fur but on top of its head, and no tail. His eyes were pale blue and his fur was yellow as sunlight in water.

I swam with him from one end of the pond to the other and back, gently because he was a weak swimmer, unlike the sea lion or otter.

Aleea called to me from the inlet. I ducked and came up under the human creature as a mother would under her calf, carrying him on my back. It tickled when he wriggled along my back to my blowhole. I stopped at the bar of pebbles blocking the inlet and told Aleea of my discovery. At first she was afraid for me, saying where there was one, there would likely be more, and perhaps they weren't all as friendly as this one. The youth must have sensed her fear. While we spoke back and forth, I felt a strong wave of feeling coming from him—concern for the two separated whales, perhaps even pity. His small body was warm by my blowhole.

Moved by his compassion but also by Aleea's warning, I swam back to the middle of the pond. There I tried an experiment. I sang several questions to the youth and waited for him to answer. After a moment he pressed his head close to my skin and replied in short, jerky sounds—not very musical.

I couldn't make out his words, but I had a strange sense of his meaning and tried to respond. When I paused, he crept close to my blowhole and breathed his song down into it while he patted me with a flipper. His breath was faint but warm. And I breathed back, full in his face.

At that moment something wonderful happened. Although I could not understand his tongue, when he uttered song, the sound made clear pictures in my head. I sang of how I was trapped and needed to get out to Aleea. He answered with a series of sounds that meant he understood. The pictures showed me that if I couldn't escape at the next flood tide, he and his father would help me.

Excited, I nearly swatted all the water out of that pond, and I thanked him from the bottom of my heart. I was delighted that we could communicate mind to mind, despite our different speech. I think he was too, for he stood and ran back and forth along my spine, making high-pitched noises that sounded like laughter.

A second later, I was sorry we'd made a sound, for I heard many little popping noises and feared that other men might be coming. Taking a quick breath, I sank out of sight while the youth scrambled into his boat.

For a couple of minutes nothing happened. I lay at the bottom of the pond, wishing I'd taken a larger breath. Soon I'd be desperate for air. Just as I decided to rise, a picture came to mind that I knew was from my human friend, showing three other men and filled with the warning: *Do not rise.*

"I have to rise very soon," I directed my thought back to him. "I need air." But I stayed down, squeezing every muscle around my lungs.

Plop . . . Plop. Small stones fell into the pond at regular intervals. I rose as quietly as I could and breathed.

"*Whoooeeee!*" I heard a man whistle, and it wasn't my young friend. Two men stood on shore, and a large shiny red thing with two eyes crouched behind a rock. The red beast made the little popping noises. The men chattered loudly, and one pointed a flipper at me. A third man jumped out of the red beast. My friend was nowhere to be seen. I ducked under.

The next time I rose, my friend was still not there. The three men stood in a cluster, chattering and waving their flippers. At my next breath, each was on a different shore of the pond, pointing a thing like a stick. I heard a sharp *crack*. Something bounced off the water near my head and whined over the waves. Dread filled me, and I sank for a long time.

But I couldn't stay down as long as I wanted because of the ton of herring I'd eaten. Slowly I inched toward the surface, filled with foreboding. Out in the cove Aleea must have sensed danger, for she gave three short whistles of warning. Nevertheless, I needed air.

I blew and filled my lungs with air. I heard two sharp *cracks*, one after the other, and a loud blast. Sharp needles of pain pierced my head near my blowhole, and something struck and tore my skin like hundreds of sharp pebbles. I sank to the bottom and, as spots swam before my eyes, heard Aleea cry out. Dark threads wove their way up through the water from where my head was cut.

So began one of the darkest days of my life and possibly the most important. I lay on the bottom stunned, wondering how the killers had found me in this tiny pond and thinking about the youth. He was gone, I sensed, for I received no pictures from him. I had felt his pity and affection, and I worried that the others had hurt him or driven him away.

Dazed, I did not know how much time passed before I rose. Again I gulped air and again two shots rang out. Once more sharp pains pierced my blowhole. *Boom*—a second blast came just as I went under, followed by the hiss of many pebbles striking the water. While I sank, more dark threads from my wounds uncurled above me. My mind was clearer though, and I resolved not to surface for a long time.

Constantly, Aleea's low song came to me, offering courage and solace, masking the panic she strove whalefully to hide. Her movements on the other side were nervous and swift, however. Steadily the old song came:

> *Whatever rocks wrack you and rise to rend you,*
> *Whatever tides tear you and sweep you away*
> *To alien shores and waves that are angry,*
> *Deep in my heart I will breathe deeply with you*
> *The breath of the one who made you and keeps you.*
> *Courage, my Heart, courage and patience.*

My head throbbed with pain, but gradually the rhythms of her song soothed it, and my pulse slowed. I knew I had to slow it further to stay under long—down to one beat a minute. This would slow the bleeding too. I pretended the pond was Hralekana's cavern with the glowing rocks where I had stayed under for surprising lengths of time.

Fortunately, the sharp pebbles had pierced only the thick layer of blubber above my skull, or so it seemed. But now these cuts started to burn in the salt brine. I ignored the pain as best I could and slowed my heart, repeating over and over a song of one syllable, ignoring all thoughts, frightening or otherwise, to focus on that one sound.

It was an hour before I rose again. On the shore were many humans and a number of the brightly colored beasts that rumbled and gave off foul-smelling smoke. I saw fire flash from the thundersticks. More shots than I could count rang out, and a roar went up. Pebbles spattered the water around me like rain. But four struck home, and this time, choking, I sucked in blood with the air. I sank before they could fire a second round.

My heart beat rapidly again as I lay on the bottom, trying to control it. Aleea called to look out above, and sure enough, three or four small boats were moving out from shore. For a moment I thought the youth had returned to help, but then I saw the thundersticks and wavery shapes of men standing in the boats.

Zip — zip — zip — one after another the sharp stones shot down into the water as I zigzagged to the other end of the pond. Back and forth the boats hunted me, and I knew no rest. Twice pebbles pierced my skin, but most, slowed by the water, bounced off. The pain was driving me mad, and once, crazy with it, I tried to thrust my way through the narrow inlet, now completely high and dry, receiving for this a lacerated chin and three shots in the flukes. With a roar, the killers ran around the pond toward the inlet while I thrashed back underwater.

Not long after, I heard the rumbling of the noisy monsters on the pebble bar. I heard the clang of rocks lifted into them and the thud of rocks thrown down on the bar. The noise went on for an hour, and when I rose again, a wall of rocks had been piled across the inlet to block any escape at high tide.

The water above me was now clouded red with the blood winding up from each wound. At times the pain was maddening, and, thrashing my tail in agony, I happened to rise close to the boats. I accidentally bumped two and sent the hunters sprawling into the water. Four of them yelled and splashed toward shore while their black sticks spiraled to the bottom. I followed the sticks down. Part iron, part wood, they looked small and harmless enough.

After that no boat came out.

But the pain and loss of blood must have made me delirious. Or I was having another Seeing. I recall a strange time, half real, in which snatches of Aleea's song came through like a refrain between Seeings. In the first, I was a Gray whale calf in this same pond. When I rose I heard a beat of *boom boom boom* along the shore and saw shapes, red and black, leaping around bright fires. Two narrow boats came out on the water, and men stuck long sticks into me. I felt the sticks go through my heart and lungs and the blood burst inside me while I screamed to the rest of the pod, helpless outside in the cove. The hunters dragged me up on shore, where they cut the flesh from my bones. What was left—my skeleton largely—they dragged out into the water, and I floated away, light and airy, seeing the sky between my bones. The Seeing passed and I heard Aleea,

Deep in my heart I will breathe deeply with you.

In the second vision, I was not in the pond, but on the other side of the ocean in a narrow fjord, where the mountain walls come together over deep waters. I recognized the fjord from the story Spygga told me. I was a Fin whale, the leader of a pod driven there by men in boats who dropped explosions in the water. A net was put over the mouth of the fjord, and we were hunted by them with long sticks in the same boats. They cut us with sticks that smelled of dead flesh—stabbed us as we came up to breathe, deep, past the blubber. We gradually sickened as the rot set in, and poisonous gas swelled in us until we were nothing but one huge pain from flipper to flukes. They let us die in this agony, sometimes for days, before they put a rope around our tails and dragged our corpses to shore.

Courage, my Heart, courage and patience.

I came out of this vision believing that I would die in the pond. Out in the cove I heard a rapid *thrug thrug* and worried about Aleea. I called to her. She assured me she was all right—hiding at the bottom—but that the boat was headed for the inlet. I heard it strike the gravel beach on the far side, and I feared it brought more men with sticks. Then a picture of a long, yellow boat flooded my mind, and I recalled the words, "My father and I will help you." My friend had returned.

Desperate for air, I surfaced again. This time there were no shots. I glanced quickly about and saw a man walking in front of the others, waving his flippers and shouting, his back to me. The others were angry and menacing him with their sticks. Walking with this man was my friend with the yellow hair. As I slid back down, my breath hung, a red mist in the air.

A long while later I felt my friend calling to me—*Rise up! Rise up!*—his thoughts sharp with anxiety. When I rose, it was dusk. Only two men remained at the pond, my friend and the larger one who had waved his arms at the killers. His father, I guessed. When he saw me, my friend cried out in tones of joy and worry and ran toward one of the boats.

I sank under and waited, halfway to the bottom. He came out quickly this time, pushing the long oars. I rose, and in a flash he was in the water stroking my side. His voice was low and sad. When he climbed on my back, he found the wounds and made a strange choking sound. I felt warmth fall from his eyes onto my skin. After a long silence, he spoke. His voice was soothing as he carefully touched the wounds.

In gentle tones he told me what he saw, and I pictured it clearly. He said that the wounds, though many, were not deep—that unless they grew infected from the pieces of metal in them, I would probably be all right. While he shared his thoughts with me, I sang them to Aleea, still restlessly patrolling back and forth in the cove. He said that certain wise men could probe into the wounds and remove the metal bits. Though I was sure he meant well, I didn't like that thought at all.

The man on shore called to him and the thought "father" crossed my mind. The youth answered, saying something about the wounds. They spoke back and forth for a while, and I realized I didn't know my new friend's name. When they paused, I said loudly, "Hralekana."

He stared at me, and I repeated my name. He looked thoughtful and said slowly, "Ra . . . Hra-la-ka-na." I hardly recognized it, so strange was the sound in his small, human voice.

"Hralekana-*kolua*," I said.

"Hra-la-ka-na *ko-lu-a*," he echoed back, the syllables short and in one small range of pitch. But he said it with love.

Then he said, "Mark."

"Hmakh," I repeated. "Hmaark. Hmark." It was a strange sound on my tongue, a gift to be treasured.

While Mark lay on my back, he shared with me what he knew about my attackers. I swam slowly up and down, keeping an eye out for any who might return, listening for their metal monsters. My wounds stung in the cool air.

He told me that the men with sticks wanted to kill me, though they did not want my flesh for food. To them it was a game. They wanted to kill me because to do so made them feel brave, though they were all cowards or they would never hurt a helpless animal. His father had been able to stop them because he had talked with the leaders of the human pod. (And I saw by *pod* he meant thousands and millions of humans—as many as swim in a bed of krill.)

The leaders had ordered the hunters to stop. The hunters were not happy about this and threatened Mark and his father with thundersticks. The hunters might make the leaders change their minds and come back tomorrow with more powerful sticks—perhaps even a harpoon. Though the law said no whales could be killed on this coast, not so many years ago there was a law that said they could be. The killers might get the leaders to change the law for one day. They had piled rocks across the inlet so I would not escape at high tide.

Mark's words were low and broken as he told me all this. Yet, he said, and his voice rose a little, the leaders might do another thing. Because I was a white Humpback whale and they had never seen one, the leaders might say no to the killers and send other humans to do certain things to me, probably harmless. These were wise humans who wanted to know more about whales. But these wise humans, because of their desire to know, would not let me go free. They would send a ship to tow me to a lagoon where they kept dolphins and other sea creatures. Whatever happened, he would be with me and do his best that I not be hurt. So would his father. But he did not know what he or his father could do if the killers returned tomorrow. Meanwhile, he hoped to come back and spend the night with me.

Mark lay there silent awhile, rubbing my back. I felt the warmth from his eyes a second time, and at last he said good-bye and paddled to shore. He and his father crossed the neck of land to their yellow boat, and I heard the whine of its motor fade.

My wounds started to throb, and I felt feverish. The dull maroon clouds in the west faded to gray. I was alone and frightened. Threads of blood still spooled from my wounds to the surface. I swam up to the inlet and stared at the immense pile of rocks and boulders the killers had placed in my way. Escape was impossible.

That was my lowest moment.

Then slowly, in a low voice filled with tears, came Aleea's song:

> *Whatever rocks wrack you and rend you,*
> *Whatever tides tear you away . . .*

I concentrated on slowing my pulse to ease the throbbing in my head and tail. I counted slowly and focused on nothing but her words:

> *Deep in my heart I will breathe deeply with you.*

During those next dark hours it was only the singing of Aleea that kept hope alive in my heart; otherwise I would have despaired, surrendering to the blackness of my thoughts. I cannot tell you what she sang, for after a while she abandoned the songs we both knew and began a new song of her own. What she said in that song sent fire and strength through me as she shared the deepest thoughts and feelings of her heart. I knew then that if I died in this pond, I would die content with what she had told me.

I must have slept, for the next thing I knew the air was cold and the sky black, the stars scattered across it like bright scales. I looked up and saw no Leaping Whale. That constellation was not visible from this side of the world, but I saw the starry image of Ohobo striding with his bright harpoon at his side. This image gave me hope, for I recalled how each time Ohobo came after us in rage, we whales outwitted him.

Then I heard again what had waked me: a splash at one end of the pond, followed by some clicking of rocks and another splash. At the same time, I heard a low call and knew Mark had returned. Eagerly I swam to the inlet. Mark was carrying away some of the smaller rocks. He waded in and placed a hand gently on my bruised upper lip.

"So, you are awake," he said. "What do you feel?"

"Pain," I sang back to him, "though my head is no longer throbbing."

The tide had risen and was only a couple of hours from the flood. The pebble bar itself was already underwater, but the rocks and boulders made an impassable wall.

"I will clear away what I can of the rocks," Mark said. "I can't do much about the boulders."

He went back to work. *Splash . . . splash*—rock after rock landed in the pond to one side. He worked for an hour, and the tide had risen farther, but the boulders still stuck out of the water like big, jagged teeth. The surface was calm and reflected the stars. A black shadow moved up on the far side of the boulders. It was Aleea. Each could see a little bit of the other's silhouette through the gaps in the rocks.

Mark wrapped his flippers around one boulder and made grunting noises, pressing his flukes against another. It did not budge. He tried this twice more and, letting his breath out in a long sigh, waded out to me again.

"Nothing," he said. "I couldn't move it one pebble's-length." There was a scraping noise behind him, and he turned. Aleea was pressing a large boulder from the other side—pushing with all her might—and it moved a little. Excited, she backed up and swam at it full speed. I cried out too late. Her jaw made a loud crunch as she rammed the solid rock. She groaned and pulled back, her lip scraped and bleeding.

Again Mark tried, this time making angry sounds while he strained. It was no use, and the water wasn't high enough yet for me to reach the boulders. Just then we heard the *pop-pop-pop* of a metal monster coming.

"Dive!" Mark yelled at Aleea and me as he ran behind a boulder to hide.

I hurried out to the middle and sank. From underwater I saw the lighted eyes of a monster pull up to the far end of the pond. The shadows of two men crossed in front. One shone a blinding light down into the water. It found me and went back and forth along my whole length. The two stood there a few minutes, then the light went off. Shortly afterwards the lights of the monster swung away, and its whine dwindled faintly through the water.

I came up and spouted. When I reached the inlet, Mark was already trying to push the rocks again.

"That was close," he said. "It was two of the killers. Fortunately, once they spotted you, they didn't shine their light toward the inlet."

The water was now almost on a level with the boulders spaced across the inlet. I tried to reach them. My belly scraped the sharp pebbles, and I thrashed hard with my flukes. At last my jaw pressed against two of the large boulders.

I pushed, and my head filled with pain. Every wound throbbed, including the three in my flukes. I stopped until the pain subsided and then pushed again. A boulder shifted an inch and stopped. I pushed harder, but it did no good.

"Wait a minute," Mark said. He ran along the shore and came back with one of the long sticks he'd used to push the boat. He propped it against one boulder and placed its end under the one that had moved.

"Now push," he said. And I did. I felt the rock begin to move as Mark leaned with all his weight on the stick. It bent like a rib.

CRACK, it snapped in two, and Mark fell against a rock. He picked himself up, limping, examining his fluke where it was cut.

"Ouch," he said, and sucked air through his teeth. I could taste his blood in the water. Without another word, he limped away and came back with the second stick.

"Let's try again," he said. And we did. This time the stick did not snap and slowly, inch by inch, we slid the boulder to one side. Aleea, watching us, smacked the water in excitement. The second boulder moved too, but Mark stared at the water and groaned.

"Quick! The tide's going out," he said. "Try to squeeze through." Thrashing with all my might, I pushed between the remaining boulders. They pinned my flippers to my side. I felt trapped and helpless. Mark frowned.

Then I thought of the killers finding me in that ridiculous position and got mad. My head was close to bursting with the pain, and that made me even madder. My whole head was on fire. I angrily trumpeted and thrashed my flukes, wriggling and slamming at that rocky bottom until one flipper, then two, made it past the boulders and pulled the rest of me along.

A second later I was free and thrashing into the starlit waters of the cove.

Mark gave a loud cheer, and an instant later Aleea was above me, examining my cuts.

"Hold still," she said, but I surfaced and turned toward the beach. Mark was standing in the water up to his knees, holding the long stick upright next to him. I swam as close as I could, and he waded out up to his neck.

"Good-bye," he said. "Go as far as you can, quickly, for they will look for you with thunderwings." He pressed his face to my lip and extended his arms along my jaw. The soft sounds of his voice flooded me: "I will come here often and think of you. Remember me."

I turned sideways and touched him one last time with the tip of my flipper and sang:

> *Wherever on the waters the winds shall find you,*
> *Wherever the moon or the sun shall move . . .*

Then he was a tiny shadow against the gray beach. Aleea and I slapped the surface and leaped once in salute— though I nearly passed out as I did.

Together we sang to him as we swam out of the cove toward the horizon, which was beginning to turn gray:

> *Hmark, O human who welcomed the whale,*
> *Who has compassion and a great one's daring,*
> *Who scathed his skin to save one from dying,*
> *Whale-Friend we hail you, brother most worthy.*

Farther down the coast a long string of tiny lights was crawling toward the pond. The killers were returning.

Before we plunged under to swim in earnest, we spy-hopped for a last look at Mark where he stood on the dark coast, holding the tall stick upright. The sight fixed itself in my mind, together with his last words, which came faintly over the water:

"I will find you again or you will find me. This is only the first of our meetings. I love you, Hralekana-kolua—Great White Whale."

Chapter Nine

WE plunged into the dark waters of the night, cool to my throbbing wounds. Aleea swam close to me, murmuring soothing words, every now and then stroking my side. She was worried. My wounds had stopped bleeding but were swollen and feverish. Though the ocean brine healed most cuts easily, wounds that swelled from within could be fatal.

We moved slowly. I was exhausted and weak from hunger, having lost what I'd eaten that morning. When at first light we reached the herring shoals, Aleea began bubble-netting, catching fish for us both. I lay quiet under the surface, trying to ignore the pain.

As the day passed, I felt stronger, though the throbbing continued. The sun sank in a clear sky as a Moon of Narrow Flukes rose in the east. Gazing at it, we heard sharp grunts to the south. I recognized their pattern. It was Spygga, and Aleea joined me in calling out to him:

> *Be well, my brother, and raise your breath*
> *Bright in the air to banner your coming.*

His spout glittered in the early moonlight, and Aleea leaped high in welcome. He looked worried as he swam up, having sensed my weakness in the water. A mile out he'd passed a white shark hot on the scent of my blood. It fled at his grunt.

While the three of us rested under the moon, Aleea told him what had happened at the pond. Spygga moved his flippers slowly back and forth, in deep thought. Finally he spoke.

"You must visit a place near the center of the ocean, called the Springs of Fire or the Fiery Trench. There, in the ultimate depth of the sea, the great land masses creep away from each other and pull asunder the ocean floor." I had never heard of such a thing, nor had Aleea, and we listened with fascination.

"Do you mean the land moves too, like the sea?" Aleea asked.

"Yes," he replied. "It too is restless, though it moves so slow we cannot see it move. The great land masses retreat from each other. So heavy is their weight they pull open cracks in the skin of the earth itself, and the inner fire spills out with molten rock. The fire warms the water and sends steam bubbling up that heals wounds. Many a Sperm whale wounded in battle with the giant squid has dived down into it for the healing of his skin.

"There is one problem, however—," he paused.

"What is it?" I asked, eager to hear more.

He looked at me gravely. "The depth is greater than that at which the broken ship lay. It is the deepest of all Deeps, and the pressure is very great—for some, too great. They are crushed by it, and fall into the Fiery Trench, never to return."

Aleea looked grieved, the moonlight glittering in her eyes. My wounds throbbed sharply.

"I will seek the Springs of Fire," I said. "If the pressure is too great, I'll return to the surface and not attempt the depths."

The next morning the three of us swam eastward. The sun rose in a fresh, pink sky, and the blue green shadows of waves slid over Aleea in an ever shifting net as she glided underwater. It struck me that this pilgrimage to the Springs might be for more than the healing of wounds. I knew before I began the Lonely Cruise that I would at some point be called to plunge to the ocean depths, there to await in silence a vision of my life. I also knew that I was not to seek that vision until called.

I hesitated to ask Aleea if she had made this plunge yet. For this was a private matter. Though the experience might be spoken of for good reason, it was often better kept to oneself and meditated upon—perhaps for years— before being shared with members of the pod.

Swimming toward the sun, I had an inkling that this descent to the healing springs might bring the vision. Though hungry, I did not eat and I spoke very little. Inwardly I sang to myself, recalling all I'd heard from Lewtë and Hrūna of the Whale of Light and the beginning of things. That last day we saw no other sea creature except one gull, crying out as he flew straight, swift, and very high into the sun. That last night we rested in a low swell under a crescent moon. Spygga said we were directly over the Springs of Fire. My wounds beat, swollen and sore.

I awoke early in the dark and breathed deeply, flooding myself with air. The others breathed with me. When the sun shot its first red gleam across the waves, I took a last breath and threw my tail high into the air, plunging straight down. Aleea and Spygga followed.

At the edge of the Black Deep I turned and touched flippers with Aleea. Though I could not see her face, I felt her grief.

With a strong thrust of my flukes, I headed down into the cold. After a while I saw far below the elongated electric fish turning like stars in the abyss. They took no notice of me as I passed and soon faded above me in the dark. The water pressed ever more heavily. I felt like a krill in the mouth of the Deep. It squeezed from all sides like the walls of a monstrous stomach while I repeated my song within me and sank deeper.

The water grew colder till I thought I could not stand it. Yet a few fathoms farther down it seemed more bearable, though perhaps I was only growing numb. The pressure increased, but the water felt definitely warmer. Night closed about me black as squid's ink, and I shuddered, fearing to meet one at this depth. I knew the great mollusks lurked here and that a whale could be caught and crushed to death before seeing his enemy.

Faintly, far below, I saw a dim whiteness waving and turning like tentacles. I stopped, then continued down cautiously. The whiteness drifted up around me. It was bubbles. Below me the whole ocean was a writhing dim whiteness of bubbles.

The increased warmth felt good, and I plunged farther, though now the pressure squeezed me like the claw of a giant lobster. The wounds on my head throbbed. Perhaps I was light-headed from the pressure, but I ceased to mind it. The bubbles tickled as they brushed against me. I dove headfirst into them, and they soothed my wounds. Soon they came too thickly to see through. The water was now warm and salty, strange with unfamiliar tastes.

Down I went, and down, as if drunk on the bubbles. The water grew saltier and hotter, and still I sank. At last I leveled off and swam straight ahead. The bubbles thinned, and I slipped out of them. They wavered and rose up in a wall beside me, a dim translucence lighting the darkness.

I looked down for the source of light. Far below in a deep canyon, a crack of fire twisted like a red river along the ocean bottom, burning bright and fading as water quenched the fire that ever bled through the skin of the earth. There was a loud hissing of steam and a violent boiling and roiling of waters. Eruptions and explosions shook the deep and spewed red lava in spouts of molten rock, sending clouds of steam bubbling upward.

The earth bled through this crack in her skin, and ruefully I knew what that felt like. Yet the steam carried to the surface life-giving salts. The wall of bubbles rose before me, stretching endlessly in the distance and far into the dark above. Among them burning gases shot up from the fires in wild colors and fantastic shapes.

I moved down the wavering bubble wall, forcing myself toward the fire below, though now the heat was as unbearable as the pressure. The wounds on my head and tail burned like streaks of lava. When I could go no deeper I leveled off, swimming into the bubble wall where it was thickest. Despite the heat, my stomach was cold with fear.

Entering, I felt myself swept away. Hot gases in the bubbles brushed over my skin like a million flippers, and the pain immediately diminished. But I was tossed nose over flukes, now sinking toward the heat below, now shooting up hundreds, perhaps thousands, of feet in a geyser of bubbles—only to sink down again. Dizzy as a herring in a bubble net, I didn't know up from down. I was swallowed by the deep, and all my movements were in vain.

At last I closed my eyes and surrendered myself to that chaos. As soon as I did, everything grew pitch black, and the motion no longer made me dizzy. I felt calm inside, and the darkness was somehow comforting.

In the darkness I saw a point of light. Slowly it expanded inside me, almost too bright to look upon. While it grew, so did music that was at once new to me and familiar, music I couldn't quite identify. The singing came from the light and wound all through me.

The light grew larger and its shape vaguely familiar. Soon it was larger than I, extending from my center beyond my skin. I was all light inside and the darkness had disappeared. The music swelled from the center, and I joined in, following instinctively the notes.

Then I heard a voice—separate from mine—speak clearly to me in the song, and it said, "*Swim.*"

And swim I did. I moved flippers and flukes, and they took hold in the chaos of rising bubbles and I swam up and down and around to the rhythm of that music. I opened my eyes and felt no fear. I saw the light within me and around me and knew I was swimming in the Whale of Light—and the Whale of Light in me.

I heard the voice a second time, and it said, *"Rejoice."*

And I did, and I felt new strength as I rose with each geyser blast and sank back toward the fiery heat, laughing with joy, reeling like a calf over the sunlit waters of a lagoon. Then, with my eyes open, I saw neither the bubbles nor the darkness but all the days of my life pass before me. And each came like a note of the music.

A third time the voice within me spoke, and it said, *"Look."*

I looked, and there was a great fire like the sun and nothing else except the glowing light all about me. I swam toward that fire. While I did, I felt a deep sorrow, though I knew not why. Tears sprang to my eyes and were ignited in that heat as they fell. My sorrow deepened and it was as if I were weeping for all things and my tears made a river. The closer I swam toward that fire, the hotter it burned. Yet I knew I had to swim into it, and I felt it sear my body. When I looked at my flippers, they were red with flame— though I could bear it and felt a strange exhilaration the closer I swam.

At last, with a strong twitch of my flukes I plunged into the ball of fire. When I did, I felt the light within me expand in an intense, white flash.

After that, it is difficult to describe what happened. It is as if I expanded with the flash and was not myself anymore. I was nothing but light, and I felt no pain and no fear. The voice was all around me and in the music, but it was as if all my senses were one sense and what I saw, felt, and heard, one thing. I could not see my skin. And there I heard things—if *heard* is the right word—meant only for me, that I dare not repeat.

The next moment all was dark, and I felt myself roll fluke over flipper in cold water. Blinking, I was in the Black Deep, and only a few bubbles spiraled lazily up under me, a dim phosphorescence in that blackness.

My lungs felt leaden. My air was gone, and I headed upwards. It was a long while before I saw the galaxies of glowing fish strung out above me. I struggled up through them, feeling only the hard constriction of my lungs and knowing that to open my blowhole meant death—though this thought did not alarm me. I concentrated on pushing toward the surface. After what seemed hours, the black lightened to gray. Then I was in the Blue Deep and a minute after that in the Green and a moment later letting out my breath. With my last thrust, I felt air and gulped it, collapsing on my back. My vision swam as two voices cried "Hralekana" and two bodies pressed against mine.

While consciousness faded, I heard Aleea say, "Look, there are only scars. His wounds are gone."

For a long time I lay there, and the others did not question me. When I opened my eyes, it was early morning of the next day. The green and silver surface of the ocean, half under clouds, was more beautiful to me than ever. Every flash of silver or white, every gleam of blue in the offing had a singular beauty, even if it existed only half a second. Each thread of cloud passing over the sun possessed a shape, a light, a color of its own that connected it to an infinite beauty.

Lying there, I made this song which I sang later that night to my friends—the Song of the Deep:

> O deep in the ocean, dark beyond telling,
> The fire burns and light keeps its home,
> Cold water scorches and hot water freezes,
> Blind fish see, for their bones are all light,
> And far from all things one is close to the center.
> Where water is heavy and crushes the bonebox,
> The heart floats light, buoyant as a bubble.
> Where the heat is greatest, healing comes,
> And far from all air, air rises forever.
> O deep in the ocean, still beyond hearing
> Sounds a voice that utters to each its own.

At last I rolled over and shook my flippers. "I'm hungry," I said. "I hope you two have found food."

"For krill's sake!" Aleea exploded in laughter and splashed water in my face.

Chapter Ten

A T dawn we swam back toward the great herring banks. I spoke little with the others, that day or the next, for I had much to consider. Some of the vision was clear, but some was a mystery whose meaning only time would reveal.

I was ravenous when we reached the shoals. Aleea and I fed side by side, and she too was silent. At the end of the second day she said, "I must continue my Lonely Cruise. You have visited the depths and had your Seeing—I can tell by your face. Now I need to seek my own. I feel it growing within me."

I understood and knew that I too must soon continue my journey around the world.

That night I had a dream of Aleea drowning far under the water. I woke, sad and restless, in the dark before dawn. Aleea was awake and ready to leave. We promised to meet again at the Ice at the End of the World. Each of us was too choked with feeling to say more. We touched flippers lightly in the darkness and then she was gone. Through the cold gray came her song:

Wherever on the waters the winds shall find you . . .

And I sang back,

Deep in my heart I will breathe deeply with you.

That night I sang the Song of Distance to Aleea and received a faint answer, which chased away some of my gloom. Again my dreams were restless, however, and I dreamt of my friend Mark standing on the shore of the cove. He was calling good-bye to me again. I resolved to visit that shore, dangerous as it was, before continuing around the world.

Bidding good-bye to Spygga, I left at night. I swam under the surface in those cold waters, watching the stars above me flash and streak through the waves. The mountains shone pink in the early dawn, but the beach was empty. I swam back and forth in the cove, keeping hidden while I waited, but soon had a clear sense that Mark was nowhere near. So I started south, following that rocky coast and passing a place where many humans lived. There were numberless boats drawn up on a beach and a large reef on shore with many lights in it. The waters stank of fish and oil. I had no sense that Mark was there either. Next morning I turned southeast out to sea and continued around the world.

Heading into the sun, I saw the black silhouette of a small sailboat cut directly across my path. Two humans were aboard. I dove and came up on the other side. One was sitting in the back, moving the wooden fluke that steered the boat. On the bow, staring into the water, lay my friend Mark. He reached down and scooped up water with something in his flipper. I spouted high and leaped, crying "Be well!" He stood up and scrambled back to his father, pointing at me. The boat came about, and in a moment they were alongside. The white hull had the image of a seagull on its bow.

That was a happy reunion. Mark wore a black skin and blue webbed feet. He leaped into the water beside me, stroking me, and shouting back to his father. Then he clambered onto my back and wriggled to my blowhole. Gently he felt my scars, questioning me while breathing down my blowhole. I sang to him of my plunge to the Fiery Trench and the healing fountain of bubbles. But I'm not sure he understood, for he kept shaking his head back and forth.

Then he spoke, and in my mind I saw the killers coming to the pond with sticks and milling around where we removed the rocks. They were angry. Next I saw him leave the place of many lights with his father in this sailboat, *The Gull.*

I couldn't picture what he said next, though he repeated it several times. At that he leaped into the water and splashed back to the boat, much faster with his new webbed feet. On board he lifted up a round shell-like thing to show to me. It was transparent like a jellyfish and held water. He took an empty one of these shells, filled it with water and put something over its mouth. He explained that he and his father collected a small amount of seawater this way each day as they sailed, and it would tell them things they wanted to know—such as how much oil was in the water from an oil spill. His father was a wise man who wished to know more about the ocean and its inhabitants in order to help, rather than hurt them. He was appalled at what other humans had done to them.

Mark took twin yellow things that looked like the floats on fishing nets and attached them to his back. (Again I was amazed at how clever he was with his flippers.) He put another face over his face and jumped in the water. He fluked and dove under me, bubbles rising as he let out air. The yellow things helped him breathe underwater. I dove—careful not to bump him with flipper or fluke—and we rolled and circled about each other, he now and then tickling me with his webbed feet.

We surfaced, and I stuck one flipper straight out. Mark swam up and grabbed it. I fluked and sank into the Green Deep with him holding on for dear life. I took him on a ride such as he had never had, spiraling down and rolling like a tentacle on the giant squid, turning fluke over flipper, and rushing to the top. All the time I sang of the Deep and of the splendid lights the Red Whale of the Sun shot down into it and how we whales freely plunged through its end-less halls forever and a day. He sang too as we did the loop-the-loop, the backspin, and the flipper-whirl, and we finished by leaping out of the water and landing on our backs. Mark sprawled across my belly, laughing.

His father brought the boat over. Lying next to it, I ate a flounder Mark had caught. While he and his father ate, I sang to them the Song of the Youth and the Whale, though I think only Mark got the full sense of it:

We roll on the surface and rock the waves wildly
And glide through the green in Leviathan wheels,
Spiraling, spinning like a circus of dolphins,
Agile as oceans of slippery eels.

Though I am of ocean and he a land creature,
Nimble and lithe, a man and a whale,
We swim like blood brothers, the big and the little,
Up through the air and over we sail.

O Mark, Hralekana-kolua now hails you,
May sun and moon bless you, each ocean you ride,
Up through the air and down under the water,
Wave-Tamer, Deep-Darer, Leaper of Tides!

I spent the day with them, and even his father climbed onto my back and examined my scars, though he would not come swimming with me. When the shadows grew long on the wave, the men pointed the nose of *The Gull* westward, toward shore. Before we parted, Mark told me he planned to go with his father to an island in the south, and then he alone would sail *The Gull* east across the ocean. It would be his Lonely Cruise, and he was excited. On that voyage, he would continue to collect water in the crystal shells.

They sailed into the purple west while I sang good-bye. I watched the sail of *The Gull* sink below the horizon, then turned to swim east under a whitish moon, now swollen to half her size.

For the next week I swam alone, straight east. I had just sighted a coast and turned south when a host of shrill whistles warned me a school of dolphins was heading my way. They leaped over me, swam around me, and played their dolphin games while keeping up a constant chatter. As usual, they had all the news of the ocean. Each member of my pod was well and accounted for (they had passed Aleea swimming south); the oil slick had broken up, after doing its deadly work; pirate whalers were hunting near the Pole; and humans in a small, yellow ship had been seen helping whales escape from them. One dolphin marked with a swirl of blue and white stayed close to my eye as we swam. His name was Stripes.

Stripes told me that the dolphins were headed for their ancient home, a sea nearly landlocked that his ancestors had left hundreds of years ago.

"It is not as deep as the great ocean," he said, "but it is beautiful. We return each year now, for the sea is changing. Each year there are fewer fish and plants in it." He looked grave and continued in a low voice. "Some say it is dying. That may be so, yet it was the home of our ancestors and is still beautiful. Would you like to see it?"

Curious about the ancient sea, I said I would, and the next day we entered a wide pass with mountains on one side and a high, lonely rock on the other. The sea was as beautiful as promised, shallow in places and sunny, and the dolphins showed me many dwellings of humans along the shore—some very ancient. Around the larger of these, the sea bottom spread like a desert, clean as a bone of any plants or fish, and rank with foul water.

But we swam among enchanting islands, and one sunny afternoon we rounded a reef to a strange sight. Before us lay the abodes of humans—underwater: ruins from which the roofs were gone, though I could still make out entrances and eyes in the ancient walls. There were smooth stone trees that at one time held up the roofs of the larger dwellings. Now these stood alone or lay broken along the sea floor.

Here and there among them moldered the remains of ships smaller than any I had seen and much older. Ahead of me, Stripes swam through an entrance and whistled. I went over the wall and through where the roof had been. In the center of the floor lay a dolphin made of stone, as large as Stripes. It was covered with sea moss, and on its back rode a human youth—also made of stone. One flipper was in the air, and on his face was the expression Mark made when he laughed.

"This is my ancestor from thousands of years ago," Stripes said proudly, nudging the stone dolphin. "At that time humans and dolphins were friends, as you can see, and they swam together through the ocean."

"It is true that *this* boy was a friend," I said. "Who made the image?"

"I don't know, but I have seen similar images elsewhere," Stripes replied, twitching his flippers with excitement. "They fell into the sea from ships. I think that people and dolphins knew each other well back then. I have even seen an image of a man living in the belly of a Sperm whale."

"That is not a very good place for a human to live," I observed.

"No. He didn't look very happy, though he was learning wisdom there. Come, I'll show you more." We swam into another large roofless dwelling. Stripes bellied down to the sand and brushed it away with his flippers. On the floor, made of thousands of little colored stones, was a picture of the ocean and many of the creatures in it: squids and octopuses, clams and scallops and dolphins, marlin and swordfish, and even a whale (though the picture of this last showed the whale with grotesque teeth and too long a tail). In the middle of all these a human stood on a giant scallop shell drawn by sea horses and by mermen and mermaids. The human who made these images, I thought, was very wise. We swam on through this reef of human dwellings, and I asked how they came to be underwater.

"According to our legend," Stripes answered, "at one time there was much shaking of the earth and fire and the rock that flows. Many dwellings of men crumbled or slid into the sea. A few, like this one, sank slowly underwater as the land subsided, and so were preserved."

That night we all rested under the stars far from land. They flashed above us as a warm breeze blew over us. Stripes nudged me. "See the Boy on the Dolphin up there?" He pointed his nose at some scattered stars that had never meant much to me. "The ancient dwellers in this sea and the humans along its shores knew they belonged together. They both felt a bond with the sea," Stripes said.

As I looked up, the constellation suddenly took shape. I thought it wonderful that what was united in the sea should also be pictured in the sky. The sky too was a sea, and the stars the shining fish of it—not unlike those that swam in the utter dark of the deep. So musing, I noticed two stars moving across the sky in different directions and faster than the others. I hadn't seen stars do this before, and the sight alarmed me. I asked Stripes about them.

"Yes," he said, "I see such stars more often all the time. They increase in number each year. I do not know what these new stars mean. They move more swiftly than the others, yet not as swiftly as those that fall from the heavens. These move across the sky at odd angles and twice in one night."

We watched the two crisscross the Boy on the Dolphin.

The next morning I said good-bye to the dolphins, eager to leave this ancient sea and continue around the world. I did stop to look at some fishing boats near an island, remembering the friendly fishermen on the herring shoals.

I surfaced near one with the image of an octopus on its bow. The humans aboard saw me and ran to the rail, pointing and speaking loudly. They had dark hair and skin bronzed from the sun and teeth that flashed white as they laughed. Taking that as a good sign, I swam alongside. Again they talked rapidly and called out to me. One threw a flounder to me, which I politely moved to take in my mouth. But while I was intent on the fish, another man took a big fishing gaff and hooked the edge of my flipper.

At the sharp pain I shook it out of his hands and flipped it over my back, diving quickly under the boat. In my haste, I bumped the boat and the man who had leaned out with the hook fell overboard.

Gliding along the bottom, I heard the engines start. Above me the boat's wake curved toward the island, leaving behind a tiny figure struggling in the water. I'd frightened the crew so badly they'd left without picking up their shipmate.

From his flailing I saw that he would soon drown. I knew that rising under him would not help, since he would never stay on my back, let alone hold on to my flipper. Remembering the sea otters I had saved, I swam up behind him as quietly as possible. He had gone under, one last flipper above the surface, when I opened my mouth and he poured in along with several tons of water.

As gently as possible, I closed my mouth on him. He gave a short, soul-chilling shriek. I lightly pressed my tongue to the roof of my mouth, emptying out the sea as I surfaced. I felt his tiny form stretched out on my tongue absolutely motionless. Carefully squeezing out the last of the water, I lowered my tongue, drawing in air for him through my baleen.

The octopus-boat was circling at a distance. I heard the excited jabber of the crew as they pointed at me. A rocky spit of land extended from the island into the sea, and I made for this. After a minute or two I felt the creature on my tongue turn over. His tiny heart beat rapidly.

When my chin brushed the rocks, I stopped and opened my mouth. On flippers and flukes the sorry creature crawled over my lip onto the first dry rock. He turned and stared at me, his face white with terror, his eyes dark and fixed, panting heavily. Behind me I heard a roar of voices and a slapping noise. I turned and saw the rest of the sailors waving from the deck of the boat and clapping their flippers together like seals.

I trumpeted once to them and dove.

I was glad to pass the giant rock into the colder, deeper ocean. I coasted south again along an arid shore, meeting no one. The stars were larger at night and my sleep uneasy. I had much to think about from my recent adventures, not to mention the Seeing given me in the depths.

One night I woke to what I thought was a cry.

Nothing. Above me the stars blazed, and a cold breeze raised a few ripples and died. With a sense of foreboding, I returned to a troubled sleep. In my dreams I saw an ancient boat with no sail or mast, the boards rotting—dead in the ocean. While I stared at it, I heard a sound like a human voice. I couldn't sleep the rest of that night, and all the following day the picture of the rotting boat with no sail clung to me like a barnacle.

The next night the dream came again, and this time Mark was on the deck, silently moving his mouth and gesturing. I woke knowing he was in trouble. The next morning, following my feeling, I turned west again. In several days I came to a strange sea, a place of no wind, the surface of which was covered with masses of brown weeds. It was a place of death, too many miles wide to skirt, and I swam under it. Every now and then I breached between islands of weeds with timbers caught in their tangles. Sometimes I saw weed-wrapped hulks rotting just under the surface, from the days when wind drove wooden monsters across the ocean. I wondered what had happened to their crews.

When I approached the far side of this dismal place, something white flashed among the weeds. A closer look revealed the tail of one white shark and the nose of a second. They were chewing on something and fled with it when they saw me. On a hunch, I breached and looked about. There, barely a mile off, a sail hung limp in the air. My heart rose to my throat. Threading the maze of weed, I swam up to a small boat with the image of a gull on its bow. The hull was scraped and battered, and no one was on deck. Feeling a terrible weight of dread, I moved alongside and thumped the hull.

Nothing. I thumped it a second time, but the hull rang hollow in that silent sea.

"Hmark!" I cried, mournfully.

Nothing but silence, stretching for miles. Then I thought I heard a faint noise below. A second later, a yellow head popped above deck, calling out my name and laughing as drops rolled down its face. Mark was so glad, he fell into the water trying to touch me. I rose up under him.

It was like old times. Mark lay near my blowhole speaking,

and pictures rushed into my head. He had left his father on an island to the west and was a week into his Lonely Cruise when the winds failed and he found himself surrounded by islands of weeds, called the Sargasso Sea. Even if the wind did spring up now, he doubted he could sail through the labyrinth of sargasso weed. The box inside the boat through which he spoke to his father at a distance was broken. Sharks circled and battered the boat for two days. He feared he would be marooned and die of thirst there—or worse. When I bumped the boat, he thought I was a shark.

At times he had called out to me from underwater, risking the sharks. Each night he prayed that I would find him. I told him how I had dreamed of his predicament and felt moved to return west. We were both silent a long time thinking of that.

At last I told him to climb on my back and I would do my best to bring him to shore, but he had a better idea. He took one of the serpentlike coils from the boat and, swimming under me, passed it twice around my body in front of my flippers. The rope was uncomfortable, but I would have trusted this man with my life. He tied the ends to the nose of the boat.

"Now," he said, "swim forward."

I did, felt the boat tug at my back, and stopped.

"Keep swimming," he said. Again I felt the tug, but kept on, and the boat behind me moved. I was pulling it. For a moment I was uneasy, until I recalled the story of

Hralekana the Great with harpoons stuck in him, pulling the ships behind him. I smiled grimly, thinking of that. How different this was that I was doing!

All that afternoon I swam between the islands of weeds, following the directions of Mark, who stood high on the bow guiding me. I steered clear of the weeds underwater, and he told me where they opened up on the surface. Now and then we had to backtrack, but together we piloted *The Gull* out of the Sargasso Sea. The air was hot and still, and the weeds smelled of rot. Toward sundown we passed the western edge. That night I pulled *The Gull* many miles north into open ocean.

We communed with each other all night under the stars. We shared our pasts and our hopes for the future. He told me that he planned to complete this voyage alone, collecting seawater for his father and sailing into the ancient sea I had visited. He wanted to learn more about the oceans and to become a wise man like his father in order to prevent other humans from hurting the life in them.

He described for me time and again his hope to sail aboard a small rainbow-striped yellow ship. This ship was faster than most and put itself between whalers and whales to protect them. The humans on this ship also saved seals from hunters. I had never seen such a ship, but the dolphins had mentioned it, and I was glad Mark wanted to sail on it.

In turn, I told him of my desire to see the rest of the ocean and to know more about humans, especially why they killed animals and plants in the sea. I told him I wanted to rejoin my pod and to see my friend Aleea. I also hoped to understand the vision I'd received in the Springs of Fire and knew I would meditate long over it in the caverns of the deep.

At dawn Mark unwrapped the rope from me and lay still by my blowhole. We were silent together many minutes. Then he climbed back aboard the *The Gull* and with one soft "good-bye" sailed into the rising sun. I sang farewell to him, leaping three times in salute while I watched *The Gull* dwindle, a black speck vanishing in light.

Then I dove and swam southeast.

Chapter Eleven

DAYS later I sighted palms on a low coast and knew I had once again crossed the ocean. The nights were warm and the stars numberless. At the mouth of a large river muddying the ocean I glimpsed a pod of Manatees, the small, shy whales who inhabit estuaries and live on the weeds there. I greeted them but they fled at my approach.

I continued south into cooler waters and eventually rounded a cape into a new ocean. Though the waters were rough and wild and the weather unpredictable, this cape was easier to navigate than the first—a good thing too, because four giant oil ships passed me. I shuddered at the thought of their breaking up in a storm. Over the next few months I explored two warm oceans and the shores of numerous islands. I improved my knowledge of underwater communication, celestial navigation, and the endless variety of creatures in the sea.

Later I visited the Pole on a side unfamiliar to my pod and befriended a number of Sei and Fin whales. I also met up with Bala the Blue again. He'd doubled in size, as had I, and again we had to part for feeding room. There for weeks among the krill I fed ravenously. My hunger was boundless, and my size and color caused comment among the other whales. Cautious of attracting the attention of whalers, I steered wide of ships—few of which were up to any good in those icy waters.

When the ice began to freeze again, I felt a keen longing for the pod. Almost a year had passed since I'd left them, so I continued on around the world toward the waters of my birth. Each day as I drew closer, anticipation mounted. I wondered which of my friends had returned from their cruises and especially looked forward to seeing Aleea. At last the morning came when a coconut floated by and I tasted in the water the islands of my birth. Soon the tips of the island mountains pierced the horizon and I called out my salutation to the others:

Be well, my brothers, and raise your breath
High in the air to herald my homecoming.

Glad was the chorus that came back to me. I recognized Lewtë's cry in it and Hrūna's. We called back and forth as I drew closer. Several miles away I breached, leaping high into the air and slapping the water.

The pod swam out to meet me, new calves and all. My homecoming was almost as good as I had imagined it. Catching sight of me, my parents and grandparents paused. Then they rushed forward, and we hugged and rolled in a typhoon of greeting. That day my happiness was complete except for one thing: Aleea had not yet returned.

"None has seen her," her mother Kaleea said, trying to steady her voice. "The dolphins have heard nothing of her since she left you at the herring shoals." I said Aleea had sought solitude after leaving me, which probably explained the lack of news. I tried to reassure her parents, but I was profoundly uneasy myself.

When we were alone together, Hrūna explained why he had stopped on first seeing me. Did I know, he asked, that I was half again as long as Humpbacks usually grew? He gazed at me reflectively. "I have always thought you would grow to great size," he said at last. "According to legend, all white whales have."

The games celebrating my return were magnificent: breaching, diving, bubble-netting, singing, tale-telling, wreath-rolling, and chain-braiding, among others that were new. When the games were over, I told the pod of some of the dangers I had passed—of the oil spill, the herring pond, and the iron whale. In return, they told me of last season's journey to the Ice at the End of the World, and of whalers now hunting small whales such as the Minke, the Pilot, and even dolphins. They spoke of a new ship of many colors that attempted to help the whales. It steered between whaling ships and their prey. Many times it came close to being rammed.

That night a full moon rose, and we joined in a gloria that lasted until dawn. The moon was so bright the schools of stars faded like herring in a murky sea. The waters calmly mirrored the heavens, while about me lay the other whales, large, with patches of white barnacles, or small, sleek, and new. Calves plunged and breached at the center of the circle, whistling as they chased each other through that huge fabric of song. Not far from the pod rose the black shape of an island from which the sweet smell of flowers and fruit blew over us, creating the ancient ache for the land.

Among those we sang were the Song of the Sun and Moon, and the Song of the Pod. But first came the Song of the Lonely Cruise. Though I had heard this one before, it had always seemed full of strange contradictions and mystery. Now as I sang it, it appeared to repeat my own journey. Last I joined in the familiar Song of the Pod:

> *When night is long and the stars are lonely*
> *And waves wash endlessly with no voice,*
> *I yearn for the pod, for the sleek sides swimming,*
> *One on each flank as we cut through the wave,*
> *For the mounting of voices under the moon*
> *In one bright chorus that rolls forever.*

When we finished, the dawn was a pink line along the horizon, and for the first time in many months, I fell asleep with Hrūna and Lewtë on one side, Hrunta and Hreelëa on the other—feeling almost as if all I'd searched for, I'd found at home.

That was a good season. Hrekka returned, larger, more serious, but still with a taste for porpoise, as we say of a mischief maker. Together we visited the lagoon of our calf-hood, as golden and warm as ever—if somewhat smaller to our eyes—and the ship graveyard. I told him of the great ship that lay broken at the bottom of the other ocean.

Several times I went alone to this place of silent, ruined ships to reflect upon the mystery of humans. They were very clever with their flippers. I knew they created these iron monsters with them, as well as the large reefs on shore, the tall towers with brilliant eyes, and the noisy metal creatures that moved on land and in the sky. No other animal made such wonderful things and so many, and yet to what end? Why did they need all of these things to eat and be happy? It seemed to me that with them they were bent on destroying the very earth and water that gave them life and happiness—if they ever knew happiness.

Despite these reflections, it was a happy time. The only shadow on the brightness of those days was the absence of Aleea. Part of me always listened for the faintest echo announcing her approach to the pod.

The scouts returned that season with news of pirate whalers, and my anxiety increased. While the waters to the south warmed under the flaming flippers of the Red Bull, we swam slowly toward the Ice at the End of the World. At night I slept uneasily and called out through the lonely canyons the Song of Distant Love:

> Now, my Love, while the waves shine whitely,
> Each to each in the moon's bright leap,
> My song goes searching till your song shall answer,
> Its word come back like the wandering wind.

I'd go off by myself, singing by the hour, pausing to listen. In the moon I'd watch the silver hair of the waves recede in endless rows over the horizon and hope that each one would bear a note to her ear. I'd listen, but all I heard was the cry of a disconsolate gull or the whisper of surf on some distant shore. Thinking of Aleea herself on such a shore, alone and desolate, listening to a gull's mournful cry, I murmured her name among the words of one of our greatest singers:

> *Perhaps this self-same song will find a path*
>> *Through the sad heart of Aleea when, sick for home,*
>>> *She swims in tears along an alien shore;*
>>>> *The same as her song has*
> *Charmed my heart, circling in the foam*
>> *Of perilous seas, by human lands forlorn.*

I repeated the last line, loving the sound of *human* and *forlorn* together, each word desolate and filled with yearning. And then my vision blurred and my voice broke as I listened in vain, hoping to hear but never hearing,

> *Surely as the sun swims after the moon,*
> *So does my heart press hard after yours . . .*

Often toward morning Lewtë would swim up beside me and persuade me to rest, continuing to listen for me while I caught forty winks.

Three days from the Pole we met a pod of Fin whales swimming slowly northward. One had been cut across the dorsal by a pirate whaler's harpoon. The others were holding him up, one on each side, fending off sharks until the wound healed. This news increased my fears, and I urged the pod on as fast as they could swim. But the calves slowed us down.

The urge to get to the ice consumed me, a sense of unspecified danger. That night I bade farewell to Hrūna and Lewtë and went on ahead, promising to meet them in several days. I swam through long moonlit corridors in that chilly water. When I passed close to Hralekana's cave, it seemed I could hear the strong vibrations of the legendary whale's chant through the midnight waters, and it only heightened my anxiety. I knew I had to reach the ice.

In the dark morning of the second day I heard a faint cry. It was a cry of terror. A shiver of fear shook me from nose to fluke, and I moved forward full-speed. It was a distress cry, one that a Humpback utters when its life is threatened. And the voice was familiar. I trumpeted as loud as I could, telling the caller I was coming. For indeed it was Aleea. Her cry sounded panicky and short, and I feared the very worst.

I plunged ahead in the gray dawn, now tinged with red. I called out to Aleea as her cries came faster. Soon I heard another sound. It was a cold, thin sound I had heard only once before, when pursued by the iron whale. It was the sound iron monsters make hunting their prey by echo. *Ping,* it came softly at this distance: *ping . . . ping* at intervals. And with the echo came the distant *thrug* of screws and the faint clang of steel moving and shifting.

Over the horizon rose three whale catchers and a larger ship with a cavernous black mouth. They were closing in a wide semicircle. The factory ship looked like a ghastly mother and the catcher ships her cruel offspring, sharp-nosed and fast. An even smaller ship trailed behind her like an unweened calf. The rising sun glowed pink along their sides and tops. Beyond them I saw a solid line, also pink, of the ice from which Aleea was cut off.

Aleea's cry came again, and I called to her to stay under as long as possible. The ships moved forward cautiously, drawing the circle tighter. A mile from them I plunged underwater. I knew what I must do. My mind was clear. I began an ancient Battle Song to encourage us both:

> *Day rises red on the running wave,*
> *Mist clears above us, ice mountains rise,*
> *When I must do battle with iron Behemoth,*
> *Flipper and fluke against unfeeling steel.*
> *My Love, if the two of us, battered in battle,*
> *Here for the last time take leave of each other,*
> *Heart shall the stronger be, mood the merrier,*
> *Head the clearer, courage the keener,*
> *Spirit the brighter, as our might dwindles.*

The hulls of the approaching whalers grew larger. I did not have much time. Soon their echo finders would locate me, and the effect of surprise be lost.

At last I glimpsed a quickly moving shadow. Aleea was swimming in nervous circles. She rushed up to me, the star above her eyes showing through the murky water.

I have never forgotten her look and the embrace that followed. Brief as they were, our whole lives were in them.

Quickly I breathed my plan in her ear. So far, I figured, their echo had shown the whalers only one whale. I told her to swim deep and fast to the ice. I would wait in her place and distract the ships until she was safe, then join her.

Aleea stared at me long and said, "I'd rather die with you than apart from you."

"There is no need of either of us dying," I said, forcing a smile. "Go! As fast as you can." She turned and sped downward. I flung myself toward the surface, in the center of the tightening circle of ships, and breached with a bellow, rising high into the air and crashing loudly on my back. Still out of harpoon range, the three catchers surged toward me.

I lobtailed quick as I could and waited until all three ships drew close, then aimed for a point between the nearest two. I leaped a second time, and the crews ran to the rails, yelling and pointing. Then I ducked under and waited. As I hoped, at the sight of the outsized white Humpback between them, the two veered toward each other. Too late they realized their error. Screws whined in reverse as the hulls floated helplessly closer. With a satisfying crunch and tearing of steel, the bow of one buried itself in the side of the other.

Trumpeting victory, I turned and sped after Aleea.

The next few minutes were chaotic, and I hope I can recall events in their right order. I looked ahead and saw Aleea's shape tiny in the distance. The shadow of the third catcher passed over her in hot pursuit and turned between her and the ice. She slowed, faltered, and started to circle back.

"Swim straight ahead!" I cried, desperate, and raced toward her, climbing to the surface. Again I leaped, a distance in front of the third catcher, taunting it. I stayed up and spouted high. The catcher turned toward me, forgetting Aleea, and I saw the harpooner crouch behind his glittering cannon. High in the water, I swam toward the large factory ship, which had lowered her jaw in anticipation of whale meat and bones. The little calf-ship I'd seen earlier was nosing out from behind her.

The sharp nose of the catcher came on fast behind me, parting the water to either side. I forced myself to wait until the last moment to dive. That was a mistake. As I threw my flukes in the air, an explosion shook the water.

I felt a stinging in my flukes as I dove. An instant later a second explosion followed. A giant clamp squeezed my head, and blackness swam before me.

I fought against the blackness, and the next few moments seemed like an eternity. A second time my life passed before me, and then the light returned. I was dazed, floating toward the surface where I didn't want to be, but my breath had been knocked out of me and I was starving for air. The next moment as I breathed, I bumped against the yellow side of the calf-ship.

"This is it!" I thought. The yellow ship was right against me—yet nothing happened. While I gulped air, my head cleared, and I noticed two things: one was the harpooner angrily shouting from the nose of the catcher where it loomed over the small yellow ship. A cable from the catcher's bow hung straight into the deep, weighted at the end by the exploded harpoon that had taken a notch out of my flukes. The other was the many colors painted across the top of the yellow ship and, on its bow, the image of a rainbow with a Humpback breaching through it.

Chapter Twelve

I DOVE and swam in a wide arc toward Aleea and the white line of ice on the horizon. As I did, the catcher's engines started again. It backed away from the *Rainbow Whale* and turned toward me. But the *Rainbow Whale* was faster and once again blocked the path of the angry harpooner. This time it looked as if the catcher was not going to stop. The large factory ship had also changed course, and her black bulk bore down on the yellow ship, whose bright colors wavered down through the water.

Sure enough, the catcher did not slow up. But the *Rainbow Whale* roared nimbly out of the way, crossing right in front of the factory ship, which slowed to a halt. Men ran to her giant nose, shouting and waving at the intruder. Now the catcher was closing on me again, though still a distance away. Glancing back, I saw the *Rainbow Whale* speed up, heel over on her white wake, and curve between us. I hurried toward the ice.

Aleea, a tiny speck in the distance, grew larger as I gained on her. While I swam, I directed my thoughts to the *Rainbow Whale*, picturing the youth Mark. But no picture returned. With an uncanny certainty, I knew that he was not aboard. I was both disappointed and relieved, while pleased that there were other humans who loved whales enough to risk flipper and fluke for us.

At last side by side, Aleea and I dove beneath the blue mountains of ice. Harsh music growled and whined about us as the icebergs jostled each other, moving toward the open sea. But that music was sweet to us while we swam under them toward a far green recess between their snowy cliffs.

Rising safe within their encircling walls, Aleea and I clung to each other, flipper to fluke, weeping from relief and joy. Through her tears, Aleea said she thought I'd been harpooned when she heard the explosion and saw me float to the top. She thought the yellow ship had come to tow me to the factory ship to be torn apart. She had decided to swim back and die with me when—miracle of miracles—she saw me dive and swim toward her.

Then she examined the notch in my flukes, still bleeding a bit, and her tears came afresh.

I explained the *Rainbow Whale* to her and told her about people like Mark and his father. I asked her where she had been the past months—telling of the pod's worry and how I'd felt compelled to swim ahead of the others to find her.

She swam over to the edge of the ice lagoon, surrounded on all sides by a dozen huge bergs. The sky shone blue above us, and a few gulls wheeled lazily. The icebergs creaked and sang. Looking back at me, she began softly:

"It feels strange to share any of this," she said. "At the time it seemed too private. It has to do with my plunge to the deep and what followed." She paused. Snow and ice slid from one of the giants, making a momentary mist in which a hint of rainbow shone. She spread her flippers wide and sculled toward me.

"After leaving you, I swam south for many days alone with my thoughts. Nothing special happened, except that the ocean seemed unusually empty. One day the sun rose, as on all others, but I knew that was the day I must descend."

She idly stirred the water, and I thought how beautiful her reflection was in its mirrorlike surface.

"After breathing deeply for a while, I dove farther than ever before, past the Blue Deep into the Black, down past the fish made of light, until I came to rest on the bottom in utter darkness. I felt squeezed and compressed, as if the bottom were a tongue pushing me against the roof of a giant mouth. And then in the darkness a sound came."

She stopped with a strange smile on her face. Her eyes glistened.

"It was a music I had never heard before, from whale or any other creature. It was deep and it was high and all ranges in between, swelling and fading like the waves. I thought it contained voices, though the voices were not clear. Still it was incredibly beautiful and I knew I had to follow it.

"I rose from the bottom and swam through the darkness, the music gradually growing louder. I followed it for a long time, sometimes veering off in the wrong direction and waiting for the music to swell again before adjusting my course. Little by little, the water grew lighter—first blue, then green, then gold. I thought the golden light above me was the sun.

At the same time I heard the loud crashing of waves on rocks and their ringing above the music.

"The light came from the entrance to an undersea cavern. I grew afraid as the currents pushed me to one side. But I swam with all my strength and entered the light-filled water, the rock ringing with music all about me. I surfaced and found myself in a cavern filled with a golden light that played over the ceiling as the waves danced beneath it. From the ceiling long teeth of stone reached down, and through the water stone teeth rose to meet them in fantastic shapes and shifting colors.

The cavern spread far back and opened out on others. The light shimmered in waves over the ceiling. It came from openings in the walls through which the sun shone, reflecting from the water. A wind moved through the cavern, and while it blew, the stone teeth hummed, and at last I knew the source of the music—or at least part of it. Gone from it now were the voices I heard earlier. Nevertheless, the music was sweet, and I listened enchanted until I fell asleep and dreamed. At least I thought I dreamed.

"In my dream I was still in the cavern, underwater, and I saw a man looking down at me from the surface, his hair floating about him like seaweed. From the middle down, his body was shaped like a fish or seal. I remember thinking in my dream how odd that was. Then I woke up. I was in the same position underwater, only no creature was to be seen.

"Deciding to explore the cavern, I swam back into it between stone teeth thrusting up from the floor. Eventually these thinned out, and I passed through a narrow entrance into a larger cavern beyond, where the light was dimmer. This second cavern soon opened into a third, where the floor fell off into darkness and a deep pool—how deep I do not know. I thought this might be an opening to the ocean under the earth. Still the music of the wind and stone hummed in the water all around me. I swam farther and farther into the cave. There seemed no end to it. While I swam, I heard faint traces of voices returning and blending with the music.

"It was then that another kind of light appeared—as if it came from inside me. I cannot say—" Aleea cleared her throat and looked away for a moment. "I cannot say what I saw and heard in that light, but I can tell you that the strange voices, so beautiful, became clear to me in our language, and what they sang was recorded on my heart.

"When the vision faded, the voices continued while I swam back to the second of the lighted caverns and out into the golden brilliance of the first. Without stopping I swam through the underground entrance to the ocean. The currents pulled at me crosswise as before. But I swam with strong strokes past the undertow, away from the cauldron of surf above, and still the voices sang out over the sound of the waves. When I was well away from it, I surfaced to breathe and lay there stunned by what I saw. Behind me was an island consisting of one tall mountain of rock. There was no shore, no beach, just jagged rocks piled at its base and cliffs soaring into the clouds. All around it breakers exploded in high spumes and geysers of foam.

"But it wasn't these that held me. There, just beyond the scrim of surf, the spindrift and mist flung high by the calamitous waves, I saw them. Stretched on the rocks, arching their tails in the spray, hair curling over their shoulders, a few pressing to them things made of shell and strung with sinew, their bright human faces flushed with joy, rested creatures like the one I'd seen in the cavern. They sang as they stroked the shells that thrummed and vibrated, and their hair blew and lifted in the wind like spindrift from the breakers ever rising and falling.

"Sharply their song came over the sea, louder than before, as if they knew I was there. And I felt the longing that had maddened whales and driven whole pods onto shore, where they died out of water. I felt their longing for the land, their desire for union with something beyond themselves. Wondering, I also recalled the legends of mariners who had heard these same songs and driven their ships upon the rocks in their madness to join these Sirens of the Sea, only to perish and drown. Perhaps in humans the sea people evoked the longing for the ocean. For the mermen and mermaids, half human, half sea creature, were united with both land and sea.

"Nevertheless, it was sweet, the sweetest music I had ever heard, and it pulled on the deepest strings of desire. The longing was for—I don't know what—and for the longing itself one would give up any number of things.

The song seemed to fulfill desire, until a new depth of desire opened under that one, so that the desiring was the having, yet the having was the desiring.

But for me their song, though sweet, held no maddening impulse, for I understood its words and had heard them as a chorus to my vision of the light, which they too waited upon and served, even as did my own song. I am not able to recall all of their song, much less to put it into our own tongue, but here is some of what they sang to me deep in the cavern and over the waves:

> Come to our mountain where land and sea marry,
> Where water and rock join and retreat
> To return again wild for the arms of the other,
> Waves ever restless and running together.
>
> O come to us here, where land and sea marry,
> The wanderer's rest, and the wild wave's,
> The bitter cold sea and the hot sun above you
> Will no longer burn where our bright hair floats over you.
>
> Land and sea, sun and moon, day and night, storm and calm,
> Depth and height, cold and heat, light and dark, wound and balm,
> Marry in the music that murmurs like a river
> Where we swim in our bright golden caverns forever.

"That music was as perilous as it was sweet, but not to me who knew the secret it hid. I turned from it and plunged into the Black Deep again until its last strains faded in the darkness. Soon I was at the bottom where I'd first heard the music. Starved for air, I swam with my remaining strength for the surface."

She stopped, and we were silent a long while, a single gull occasionally crying out above us.

At last I said, "We must warn the others of the whalers." We plunged back toward the edge of the ice, swimming under those blue and emerald mountains that sang to us of the warm sea, the sky, and the perfect cold above the Pole, where they were born as tiny crystals. We didn't say much but gazed at each other, eye to eye, flipper to flipper, while we swam. Words were unnecessary, for we knew without saying it that neither ever again wanted to part from the other.

Outside the ice I surfaced to look for the whalers. The damaged catcher was close to sinking, its stern just a few feet out of water, and the men still aboard were climbing along ropes to its sister ship. The factory ship and the third catcher had sailed west and were half below the horizon. We waited by the ice while the second catcher took aboard the rest of the crew and retreated after them. The little yellow ship was nowhere in sight. Turning in slow circles, the damaged whaler made a loud gurgling sound as its sharp bow rose in the air, harpoon cannon shining in the sun, and sank. Bubbling up after it, oil and other flotsam stained the clear green sea.

Aleea and I skirted wide around it and swam back the way I'd come. When we met the pod that afternoon, there was great jubilation over our safe return. You'd think a squall had blown up the way the waves rocked and danced from the breaching, slapping, and rolling. Finally, Hrūna called to us to save our strength for the remaining day's journey. Though the damaged whaling fleet had sailed west, the move might be a trick, and the pod must approach the krill beds cautiously.

The next day as we neared the ice, Aleea sighted three dark specks moving rapidly toward us from the west. Their movements were familiar, and soon we all leaped to welcome Ala, Ali, and Ross. The albatrosses had been searching for us and were alarmed when they passed over the whaling fleet the night before. The two older birds landed on Hrūna and Lewtë, and Ross landed on my back. While Aleea and I told him of our adventures, he helpfully pecked away at barnacles.

Now that the albatrosses—the eyes of the pod—were there to watch over us, Aleea and I left for the krill beds. For three days we swam through the krill, tunneling as we fed, making up for the lean meals of recent months and reminiscing about the rich herring shoals.

Our hunger satisfied, we said good-bye to the pod and swam toward warm waters side by side. We were going away to tie our breath together so that henceforth, wherever we were, we would swim one journey through the ocean of life.

One night, by the black silhouette of an island in a sea that lay like beaten silver under the moon, we wreathed our spouts together in the ancient ceremony. The scented air of the tropical shore washed over us where we swam just beyond the reef. A million points of light glittered from the waves as we began our wedding song, blending our voices and our lives while we sang, each to the other.

171

While the moon rose higher over that silver ocean, we swam side by side, waves foaming and sparkling over us, our voices unwinding and filling the sweet air over that empty sea—alone, except for one bird crossing the moon. The song recounted our earliest lives and our first meeting in the shadows of our mothers, our carefree childhood, and our parting as each went forth on the Lonely Cruise. It celebrated what each found alone, and what we found together as we faced the killers in the pond and, later, the whalers. It celebrated our partings and our reunions. Finally, it reached a crescendo in the Song of the Joining of Breath. From deep within, my song welled up:

> Where are you, Love whom I long for in moonlight,
> Your side flashing silver as you sink in the sea?

And Aleea answered, her high notes descending to meet mine:

> *I am here, my Love, just under the surface.*
> *I am here where I hide in the swell of the wave.*

And I again,

> O come, My Love, for the Moon lifts her flippers,
> For the Moon pours her light on the points of the sea.

And she,

> *Alas, my heart is too heavy with longing,*
> *It is hard to rise up on the wandering wave.*

And so we continued, first one, then the other:

O let the moon flood you with light leaping lithely,
O let the light carry you quick to my side.

I come, my Love, for my heart draws me to you
As sure as the flood tide cleaves fast to the shore.

Come, let us breathe our breath brightly together,
Come, let us weave a mist white with the moon.

I come. We shall spin our breath—one spout forever,
One mist forever mounting up to the moon,
Rising and falling under the moon.

While we sang our wedding song, we wove our breath together under the moon. The song went on, growing ever more elaborate and involved, till the ocean rang with it.

When we fell silent, it seemed the echo of our song came back to us from the distant caverns of the sea even more beautiful than it went forth.

A light grew in Aleea's eyes. "Listen!" she said, "the voices." While I listened, I knew this music, rich and strange, was not just the echo of our own. I could not make out all the words, though they spoke of sea, wind, and tide—of our marriage, of the marriage of day and night, sea and land, sun and moon—of the universal wedding of all things.

"It is," Aleea spoke in a whisper, "the sea people: the mermaids and mermen."

Come to this mountain where land and sea marry,
Where water and rock join and retreat

To return again wild for the arms of the other,
Waves ever restless and running together . . .

While the sea murmured with their song we began the dance, lightly slapping the waves with flipper and fluke, gently nuzzling and touching each other, turning away to dive into the deep, where we swam to each other guided by our song and by the white star on Aleea's forehead. There we clung as we rose ever faster toward the surface, singing as we breached fathoms high into the air under that westering moon—parting and falling to the waves. Lightly caressing, we began again and dove into the Deep once more and clove to one another as we rose singing out of the water high over that brilliant sea.

Finally exhausted, we fell asleep cradled in those tropical seas while the moon, washed by the waves to a pale shell, slipped under and the faint chorus of the mermen sped far beyond us to fall at last in a whisper on a thousand shores.

We spent a cycle of the moon among those islands, avoiding the occasional small sail that made its way between them. It was a moon to ourselves, out of the seasons of the pod and out of the swing of the tides, as we floated, each coming to know and celebrate the being of the other. It was a time of waves and sky and cloud, in all of which we saw the other reflected and heard our blended music. At night under the moon we wove our breath together, rolling and braiding our wakes over the dark waves, flinging the bright spindrift to the stars.

Chapter Thirteen

Swimming slowly back toward the pod at the End of the World, we passed waterfalls drifting like spume down tall cliffs. We spent days rolling in their cold, emerald waters and sending the spray high into the air. Singing, we slapped the water with our flukes, splashing each other and making rainbows, just as we did when calves.

When the seas grew colder, we swam faster, eager to rejoin our friends and feast upon the krill. Long before we reached the Pole we sent our Song of Greeting under the sea. The glad voices of the others came back in a chorus, singing the Song of the Newly Joined to us, which ended:

> Through daylight and darkness, through storm and calm,
> Through want and plenty, two swim as one.

Our parents and grandparents swam out to us and solemnly embraced us with outstretched flippers.

Soon we were back in the thick of the krill, an ocean of food. How sweet it was to feed all day side by side, and at night to lie together under the polar stars, the Leaping Whale lifting bright flukes over us as he swam toward his distant star, flinging spray across the heavens.

It was toward the end of such a night that lights appeared on the horizon. Aleea nudged me awake to see in the distance the red and green lights of an iron monster. I sounded the alarm and the pod swam for the ice, for we thought a whaling ship had found us. Yet if it was a whaler, it was like none we'd ever seen. The nose of this ship stretched a great distance from its tail, and there was nothing on deck except at the stern a small white mountain with eyes. I recognized it as an oil ship, but I'd never seen one in these waters before. Sensing danger, I urged the others to flee far under the ice. The Council of Elders stayed back with me to watch the ship.

Strangely, the ship headed directly toward the ice, though no way lay open for it there. I felt more and more uneasy. Only a few miles off, it did not slow or change its course a herring's width but came steadily over the cold sheen of waters reflecting its lights. The water broke in gull's wings before the bow as it sped toward us. Did it hold some new weapon that humans had devised for our destruction? I knew the pod could retreat a mile or more under the ice, but still I felt alarmed.

Effortlessly the bow of the giant ship pushed small ice floes out of the way. Sharp cries rang over our heads as the albatrosses flew down from their snowy perch.

"Its an odd ship," Ala said, hovering just above Hrūna's head. "I can see no men moving about on it. They must all be inside."

On it came, headed straight for the ice. I had the feeling that I'd seen this somewhere before. Then I recalled the broken ship on the bottom of that other ocean and what

Spygga's grandfather had seen. This ship too was choosing to do battle with the ice—but why? Though it looked large enough to challenge even the giant icebergs, I knew their true size under the surface.

On it came, with the *thrug thrug* of giant engines. We swam along the ice pack's edge well out of its way, before turning to watch in fascination and fear. Without any lessening of speed or altering of course, it came on until barely half a mile separated it from the dark icebergs that groaned and shuddered as if afraid of the monstrous lighted shape. Still there was no sign of any man on deck, no sign that anyone there watched and knew where the ship was headed. I feared for those under the ice and hoped that none lingered near the edge.

Thrug thrug—the engines churned the sea into a mass of vibrations. Red and green, the lights shone port and starboard, and its phosphorous wake rocked us as the ship passed broadside. Brightly lit, the white stern glowed against the graying east.

On it sped till only three whale-lengths remained between it and the closest iceberg. Then two . . . then one. With a shock that shook the ocean, rocking the ice all around, the nose of the ship disappeared in a spume of mist and a thundering avalanche of ice. The sound was that of a hundred icebergs shuddering and cracking all at once. Above this we heard the twisting and screaming of steel. The front of the ship rose into the air along the face of the ice, squashed flat where the broken bow scraped and whined. It settled back with a great sigh, and a large wave rushed out from the ship, lifting us up and setting us down like so many bladders of kelp.

A harsh, repeated squawk like the cry of a demented gull came from the ship, and dozens of men ran everywhere on the lighted top. They were shouting and scrambling, while some lowered tiny boats to the water.

Relieved the ice had not given way and fascinated by the spectacle of the men, we failed to notice what was happening by the bow. We tasted it in the water before we smelled it or clearly saw it. Then, as the gray sky lightened, we watched the dark thing hump and slide, uncoiling from the smashed bow, and spread over the waters.

It was oil.

I called out to those under the ice what had happened. It was not long before the oil, coiling and shining where it crawled like a serpent from the broken bow, flattened out and snaked toward us in a dark stream. Knowing that it would not penetrate the ice field, at least for a while, I told the Council to dive, and we joined the others far within, in a green haven among the icebergs. Though we were safe for the moment, my heart was sick.

I told the pod about the other oil spill on the cape. I instructed them to swim underwater to the krill beds and not to surface where the slick had spread. Once there, we would feed as long as possible before the oil reached us. Fortunately, the end of the season was near, and we would be leaving before the new moon anyway. But I recalled the deadly waste left by the other spill. When I explained what the oil could do, the rest wondered if humans were out to destroy the ocean. Remembering that other great ship on the bottom, I said no, the men didn't intend to strike the ice or spill the oil. I believed they were swimming with their eyes closed.

On the way out to the krill I surfaced and was surprised that the ship had not sunk. It actually floated higher in the water in the bright morning light, and the worm of oil glistened and twisted as it crawled from the tanker's belly. It spread out in dark rainbows, its many tentacles like a squid's reaching over the waves. The air shook with the sound of thunderwings hovering over the ship and flying to and from the horizon. There were a few small boats in the water, but most of the crew was still on board.

That day and the next we burrowed and gulped our way through the remaining krill. Slowly the oily tentacles reached out for the krill-bed and where they covered it, the creatures sickened and died. Krill near the oil, though still alive, were tainted. Any who ate them vomited.

As the days passed, the spill spread like a giant shadow over the sea, coating the edge of the ice and smothering most of the krill. It was soon miles wide and reached far out into the ocean past a group of islands where birds nested by the thousands. Many of these were caught in it and died.

We were about ready to leave the krill beds for warmer waters when Ala and Ali, who'd kept watch every day and reported where the oil spill was going, flew above us, shrieking and carrying on. We couldn't understand the one for the other, but it was clear that Ross was in trouble. My heart rose to my throat.

"Ross," Ala gasped, "is in the oil. He can't fly." He described how Ross had been helping oil-soaked terns to shore, carefully lifting them out of the slick and laying them by their nests, when he slipped off a rock into the sludge. Trying to get out, he only flopped in deeper and was close to drowning in the coated water.

Before anyone could speak, I was on my way to Ross, the two distraught parents circling and crying above me. Aleea and Hrūna followed, calling after me to be careful. Weaving around the oil's tentacles, I saw the low rocky island, whitened with birds, who now had no water to fish in. The spill surrounded them for miles.

Taking a deep breath, I swam under the slick. The water tasted queer and burned my eyes. I circled the island, looking for anything along the shore resembling an albatross. Nothing.

The second time around I saw the edge of a rock move slightly. I looked again and saw the tip of a wing flutter weakly. A large wing. My heart, heavy as a stone, rose a little, and I surfaced as near as I could.

As I broke through the top, I felt the slick cling to my back like a giant jellyfish. My vision blurred and burned. Though I had kept my blowhole closed, when I breathed, oil crept down it like fire. All around me I heard the pitiful cries of birds trapped in the sludge calling out to their silent mates.

I heard a low croak.

"Ross," I shouted. "Is that you, Ross?"

"Hralekana?" came back a weak, scratchy voice.

My heart bumped my backbone. I surfaced and turned my tail to shore, edging it blindly toward the voice.

"Yes, Ross. I'm here. Can you see me?"

"Is that oily black-and-white rock you?"

"Rock? Which rock?"

"The one that wasn't there a moment ago. The sun plays tricks through this stuff."

I lifted my flukes a bit.

"It's you. It's you, all right!" his thin voice cracked.

"Can you climb aboard my flukes?" There was a soft splash, and I felt something brush the edge of my flukes, followed by a sad croak.

"It's no use," came Ross's voice, very low. "I don't have the strength to climb. This stuff does funny things to the head. It feels like the sun's burning me."

My heart dropped a fathom, but I called out cheerfully, "Try again, Ross. Wait, maybe this will help." I paddled backwards, scooping the edge of my flukes under the shallow water. Something soft bobbed against them.

"I'm over you," Ross called. "I'm floating over you." Carefully I curled my flukes and bit by bit raised them out of the water. There was a small weight on them.

"I'm on," Ross called out. "I'm on."

"Can you walk to my blowhole?" I asked.

"I don't know," he said. I felt his feet scrabbling. So I gradually raised my flukes and tail higher, inclining them toward my head. I kept my eyes closed against the oil and hoped that Ross wouldn't slide off. Weakly, with many a wing flop and scrabble, he slid zigzag up my back. It seemed an hour before he was at my blowhole, gasping weakly.

"What next?" he asked.

"Hold on to the edge with your beak," I said. After what the oil had done to my blowhole, Ross's beak clamped on its soft edge felt like hot pincers. But I was never so glad for a pain in all my life.

Slowly I pushed our way back through that slick with my eyes closed. The oil gave way grudgingly, tar sticking to my flukes, my lungs burning. I was guided by the calls of the pod and a joyful Ala and Ali crying out from above. But I will never forget the many cries of the birds still trapped around us, never to escape that oily grasp.

We broke into clear water, and I opened my eyes. They still burned and I had to close them again, but little by little they cleared. The pod was all around us. Aleea and Hrūna steadied me on either side while Ross let go of my blowhole. We were so glad Ross was out of the oil, we forgot he was still in grave danger. Only after Ala and Ali flew down to examine him did the celebrating stop.

"Spread your wings," I heard Ala say.

"Now, can you flap them?" asked Ali. "Is that all you can move them?"

"Yes," said Ross. I lay still while the parents attempted to clean the tarry sludge from their offspring's feathers. I felt them pull and fuss above me.

"Try flapping them now," Ala said. There was a weak flapping sound followed by silence.

"I'm afraid we'll have to wait for it to wear off." Ala was trying to sound calm, but I heard fear at the roots of his words.

"We must still try," Ala said, her voice close to cracking. Carefully they moved Ross to Hrūna's back and I fluked, breaching over and over, trying to remove the sludge that clung to my head and back. Lots of the tarry stuff slid from my skin, but I still felt coated with it, and my blowhole burned for days. I dove to the bottom and swam upside down, scraping my back against the rocks.

When I came up, Ala was high above us, gazing intently northeast. Suddenly he cried out and descended in a rush.

"I'm not sure I believe my own eyes," he said. "But on the island beyond this one there are humans. And it looks as if they're cleaning oil off birds."

"Maybe they're going to eat them," one of the whales said.

"Or steal their feathers," suggested another.

"Let's both look," Ali said to his mate, and they left poor Ross spread-eagled on Hrūna's back and flew off to investigate. In a quarter hour they returned. It was true: humans were lined along the beach putting oil-soaked terns and gulls into five large shells. These came out clean of oil and dried in the sun. A few had even flown away. The humans had already washed two sea otters and a family of penguins.

Three of us swam off with Ross, his parents circling overhead. Approaching the second island, we saw humans along the shore picking up birds. Around a rocky cape a yellow object appeared, floating in the island's small bay. My heart beat faster. It was the *Rainbow Whale*.

"We can trust these humans," I sang out to the others. Still cautious, Aleea and I went under. Meanwhile, Hrūna eased into shore, only his blowhole out of water, with the bedraggled Ross clinging to it. Hrūna might have been a piece of driftwood floating to shore. When he scraped bottom, he turned and, exposing just a bit of his back at a time, urged Ross along it toward his flukes. Ross perched unsteadily on these while Hrūna slid backwards till the half-revived bird was in a foot or two of water. With a yawp Ross splashed and waddled onto the beach, collapsing in a heap.

The noise of his splashing drew three of the humans to him immediately. Gently they lifted Ross and carried him to the large shells where, wing by leg by tail, they dipped him and worked to clean his feathers. It took a long time, and his parents circled above them, shouting encouragement. Several people stared up at them.

Meanwhile Hrūna had slipped back to us. Lying low in the water, like three rocks along that shore, we watched for hours while Ross was progressively cleaned and dried. At last his enormous wings stretched out white and clean in the sun. He ran a few steps and stumbled. Picking himself up, he tried again and after a few flaps was airborne. He wobbled twice around the island while his parents screamed with delight, swooping above him. At last he climbed smoothly, and the three flew off, the humans staring after them.

The pod rejoiced with the family of albatrosses. Over the next few days the older whales did their best to rescue terns, plovers, shearwaters, and gulls on the edge of the spill, often taking the frightened creatures in their mouths and depositing them at night on rocks near the *Rainbow Whale*. The younger whales fed on what remained of the vanishing krill.

More ships and men crowded the waters, and we soon left for warmer seas. The albatrosses flew with us until we were well away from whalers and ships heading for the oil spill. When the time came to say good-bye, I fought back tears. And for once the noisy Ross couldn't say a word.

Chapter Fourteen

WHILE we swam toward the islands of my birth, I pondered the oil spill. I wondered if fumes from the oil had entered my brain, for I couldn't sleep at night. Scenes of the dying gulls, terns, shearwaters, plovers, petrels, and corries haunted me. Not to mention the seals and penguins. After several nights I knew what I must do. I had not been to Hralekana's cavern since before the Lonely Cruise. Inside I felt a strong desire to go there and sort out all that had happened, especially the vision granted me during the Plunge, most of which I still did not understand. I hesitated to go, for the pod needed me.

Aleea read my thoughts, for as we drew near to where I would have to turn aside for the cavern, she suggested I go there.

"I know the oil spill is still with you," she said, running her flipper over my blowhole and the old scars from the killer-sticks. "I will stay with the pod while you go to the cavern and think about what all this means for the rest of us." Relieved, I told Hrūna, and later that day I quietly veered off from the others. A mile away I stopped and watched their spouts dwindle and fade into the horizon.

I felt a strange thrill of homecoming as I sped along the green sunlit corridors to the place I must dive. I was returning to the spot where I'd spent hours dreaming of what it would be like to cruise around the world. Now I had done that and was bringing back the experience to mull over in the depths.

I took a large breath and went down, remembering how I felt the first time Hrūna took me to the cavern. A dim light shone as I approached the entrance, growing brighter as I passed the threshold into that cave of luminous rocks. It was so very quiet it seemed the rocks were listening, waiting to hear something. I sang a word or two just to break the silence. They echoed and whispered from the far recesses of the cave. Turning to face the entrance, I settled down.

Lying there, I thought of the word I had always sung to collect my mind. Softly I began to repeat it, trying to slow the thoughts that raced through my head. Over and over I said it—clinging to the word and watching my thoughts rise up. I did not hold on to them but imagined them rising from the cave like bubbles dwindling toward the surface.

There were inviting thoughts: thoughts of coming to this cave before, of Aleea and our time together under the moon, of love for her and the pod. Along with these came perplexing thoughts: what would I do with my time in the cave; should I be here or with the pod; what good was this solitude? And under these burst up, violent and difficult to let go, fearful thoughts: fears for Aleea, for the pod, for our food supply at the Pole, for all the creatures poisoned there, for the whales' future. Any other time I would have taken hold of such thoughts and followed them for hours.

Now I let them flash away like herring escaping a bubble net.

Again my word resounded in the cave — and again. The echoes and whispers combined like a chorus in that place so that I hardly felt alone. It was as if all the times that word had been uttered were occurring now, as if the whole line of whales that had lain in that ancient cavern over the centuries, male and female, were chanting with me in a single moment out of time. It was as if all times sang together in chorus.

I had the distinct feeling that the world had shifted and opened, revealing that all times are one time, though we experience them one after another. Our sense of past, present, and future was merely the way we perceived time — especially our sense of the fleetingness of the moment. In this reality all moments of time opened out as present and eternal.

The voices gathered around and supported mine in countless numbers. I felt whales, as large or larger than myself, as numerous as stars in the sky, surround me in a solemn chant. I seemed to glimpse their hoary and barnacled sides moving about me. The voices rose under mine, male and female, and pressed in from both sides and gave me strength. From above, their voices reached down and lifted mine, so that for a moment I saw the words rise as bright sounds into a world of light. Then the light was inside me and filled me, and I became the shape of one sound pronouncing itself as it rose where all blended to one sound, one light. Again and again my whole body pronounced that sound.

This was all going on inside me while I lay facing the entrance, with the stones radiating dimly around me and one lazy piece of weed, caught on a stalagmite, shifting back and forth in the slight current.

I opened my eyes and was distracted by the weed. Again I wondered if Aleea and the pod were safe, and thoughts about the vulnerability of the calves, about the poisoning of our food at the Pole, leaped before me. I was pressed by a sense of urgency and had almost followed these thoughts, when I shifted my inner eye back to the word and watched while they floated out of immediate focus. Again my attention was swallowed by the simple word and its myriad echoes from the walls of the cavern, and I was content.

Again the voices pressed around, lifting me until the whole cavern was one sound, one mouth, uttering its orison to the ocean, calling from the heart of the earth to the endless waters, blue and white, that clothed the planet—the round earth itself a unique word in that mouth which pronounced it and the luminous language of the stars.

While the stars shone on the inside of my skull, like repetitions of the word gone forth to fill the void, I opened my eyes. Only the word, the simple word, remained, echoing through all the chambers of my head, heart, and lungs, the water before me still and faintly lit.

I went on, quietly repeating it, nourishing as some precious morsel in my mouth, chewing it as I watched the silent rocks and the dark deeps before the entrance to the cave. A great calm descended upon me. The thoughts that distracted me earlier ceased, as well as the visions and imaginings. Everything was simple: the word was small, and I was small. I dropped it like grains of sand, one after the other, into an infinite deep.

After a measureless time had passed in this utter simplicity, three Seeings opened out to me. Each began as a tiny picture in my brain and expanded until it was a world containing me. The first was an oil spill. I recognized the dark sludge winding its way like a huge eyeless serpent across the blue water. In this Seeing the sky was gray with an impenetrable mist, and the serpent writhed and expanded until it covered all the blue waters of the earth, until it circled all Ocean and its mouth met its tail. I saw that there was nothing but sludge and chunks of tar along every coast, and there were no weeds under the dark water and no green thing along the shore. The beaches were filled with scraps of steel and all manner of broken things, but no trees grew—all was rock. The dwellings of men were empty and lifeless, and few of the dwellings' eyes shone at night. Worst of all was the silence; there was no sound along the shore. No bird sang, and no surf washed the rocks. There was only the slow, greasy rising of the tide and its sluggish retreat.

As quickly as it came the picture faded, and a second took its place. In this one I saw our krill beds marvelously restored to freshness and bounty. In the distance, sailing over them, came three ships the size of factory whaling ships. Each of these had its mouth open and, as I watched, scooped up krill, taking ton after ton, straining it out of the sea. Where they passed, none was left. Behind them swam three whales whose blubber had long since shriveled from starvation: a Humpback, a Fin, and a Sei whale, so thin and bony they were hardly recognizable. The three swam by me in the empty wake of the ships and made no cry.

This picture too faded, and the third was a long time coming. In it I saw something large and shining in the Deep. Diving down, I found a large object round as a sea urchin that stood on the bottom. It filled me with dread. I forced myself to swim close to the device, though my whole body cried out to flee. Its skin was metal, and it made a faint—a very faint—humming sound. Something deadly came from it—something I couldn't see or taste or smell—but nevertheless lethal. In the Seeing I turned and fled from it. A deadly white fire and a waste sea spread behind me as fast as I swam. The fire caught up with me and passed me, killing everything in its way. In one moment we had circled the globe, and the waste sea had eaten up the whole world. There were no fish and no green things on the bottom—all was dead and white as bone. All the land was withered too, and the waves were pale and gray. When I called, there was no answer; I was alone in the world. The sea was waste and empty, waste and void. A deathly white surf pounded at the rocks.

The third Seeing faded, and I was back in my cave, everything still, the water dark before me, my word dropping into the silence. In the calm I considered the three Seeings, and I understood two of them, but not the third.

The third pictured an evil I could not comprehend, and yet it was the worst evil of all.

I lay there long days in that lucid calm considering the Seeings. I saw that the world need not end as it had in my visions. I thought of Mark and the *Rainbow Whale* and the cleansing of Ross, and these things gave me hope. Long I considered them and was moved to make several songs about humans and whales, which I released to the ocean currents.

I fell quiet again, repeating my word. At one point while I was fighting sleep, I thought I heard a voice whisper, *"Hralekana-kolua."*

I thought maybe I'd dreamed it, and I didn't respond.

"Hralekana-kolua," it came again, this time louder, but still in a whisper. It came from just behind me. I turned, but no one was there. For a moment I thought it was the voice of my namesake, whose presence I'd sensed while chanting, and I shivered. Was the cave haunted?

"Hralekana-kolua!" This time it was no longer a whisper, but it was in me and all around me. I *had* heard this voice before, and there was no mistaking it. I thought the rocks were growing brighter, and then I knew it wasn't the rocks.

"Yes," I responded. "I'm here."

The brightness increased right before me, and suddenly I *saw*—and I closed my eyes. I felt tears come, and I recalled words sung over a century ago:

> *The Light whose smile kindles the Universe,*
> *That Beauty in which all things work and move.*

197

"*Hralekana-kolua,*" the voice said gently. "*Do you understand the Seeings in the cave?*"

"I think I do," I answered in a small voice, my eyes closed tight.

"*Do you understand that these pictures are of what might happen? And that the third picture is the worst?*"

"Yes, I do."

"*And do you understand that humans must make a choice? All the world lies in their flippers?*"

"Yes."

"*The youth Mark is one of those who have made the choice. Guard him well.*"

At that, I opened my eyes a crack. The light was too brilliant to look upon directly, but at its center I saw the Whale of Light, and the love in those eyes cut through my heart like a harpoon.

"Yes," I said, "I will."

And then, without a word, the Whale showed me the meaning of my vision by the Springs of Fire.

At last the light faded, and I was left alone saying my simple word.

Chapter Fifteen

How many days I had been there I did not know, but at last I felt I must leave and join the others. Carefully, a fathom at a time, I rose to the top. I still felt no strong need for air and wondered at this. It was broad daylight when I broke the surface and swam toward the islands of my birth. Despite the speed of my journey, I felt calm within. It was as if I were still in the cave, and the word repeating itself over and over. In all that happened later that underlying peace stayed with me.

Yet, closer to the surface of my being I felt a strange uneasiness. At the time I thought it was the aftereffect of the visions and dismissed it, though it hung like a cloud at the edge of consciousness.

Three nights later I heard the songs of the pod unspooling along the floor of a sea canyon. From these I guessed all was well with them, and my spirits rose as I followed that beacon home.

When I reached the islands, calving had already begun. That was a good year for the pod: four females and three males were born. Aleea had a new little sister who looked as if the salt had dried on her from stem to stern. Hrēta was a lively calf, butting many an unsuspecting belly and leaping with a squeal over napping grown-ups. The numerous young needed all the more vigilance from the adults.

But it was also the season for games and for the gloria under the moon, as well as showing off for those harmless humans in small boats who came out from the islands to watch us. Some of these swam in the calm waters with us, using removable webbed feet like Mark's. The sight made me long for another meeting with my friend, but I knew he was half a world away. Meanwhile, the duties of the Council of Elders occupied me, as did renewing old friendships and making new ones.

Now and then Aleea and I would escape from the happy tumult of the pod and swim off among the islands to sing and breach together and to listen for the song of the sea people.

The weeks went by quickly, full and almost free of care. Yet now and then at night I'd find myself suddenly awake, and under that black sky with its glittering reaches of stars, the sense of uneasiness returned sharp enough to suggest danger. I worried about my friend on the other side of the world, or that the krill would not recover from the oil soon enough to feed us, or that it would be harvested by humans. Often Aleea woke and talked to me until I went back to sleep.

Close to the end of the season Hrūna called the Council together and selected me and three others to scout for krill with him at the End of the World. This was a difficult mission, he explained, because of the loss of the krill last year. We might need to seek new beds, which could mean danger and delay. We knew that the mothers, depleted by their hungry calves, needed to be certain of their annual feeding. All of us had to find krill to survive another year. He chose Aleea to go too, and we were pleased we would not be parted by the journey.

We left the next morning amid a chorus of good-byes. When the last well-wisher had leaped behind us, we settled into serious swimming, silent among ourselves. At mid-morning we heard the throb of engines and prepared to dive and skirt the iron monster when something prompted me to spy-hop for a good look. Sailing west, the sun directly over it, steered a small ship with bright colors emblazoned across her top. She was the *Rainbow Whale*, her paint new and shining, and I called out in joy. The others rose, eager to see the craft that had saved my life and Ross's. The five of us breached in unison, and the sound of that brought the crew running to the deck. We lobtailed and swam under the ship, repeating our salute on the other side. The *Rainbow Whale* slowed and circled, and I felt increasing excitement.

She stopped dead in the water and I swam alongside. Among the half dozen faces on deck was one with yellow hair and blue eyes. With a shout Mark leaped overboard, webbed feet first, and in the twitch of a fluke was on my back laughing, patting me with his flippers and calling down my blowhole. So glad was I that I thwacked both flippers and tail on the water, while the faces along the rail laughed. Aleea, Hrūna, and the others watched our reunion and continued to roll, breach, and slap the water, singing the Song of Greeting.

Soon two or three other humans were in the water.

While the small froglike creatures swam among us, we played games, giving them rides on our backs or rolling while one clutched a flipper. Hilarious shrieks and cries burst from their mouths, and we wove these into our singing of the Song of the Games.

Several of us swam over to the *Rainbow Whale* and looked at her closely, inspecting her hide from head to tail. The yellow skin was free of barnacles and wonderfully smooth to roll against. With the screws not turning, it was safe to do that. Never before had any of us felt an affection like this for a ship, almost as if she were a living thing. When we slapped flippers against her, the hull made a loud ringing sound.

Mark and I swam off together and talked quietly. There was much he wanted me to know and much I wanted to share with him. Listening to the murmur of his voice, a clear picture of the oil snaking over our krill took shape in my mind, together with the *Rainbow Whale* anchored near the island and her crew cleaning oil-covered birds. I learned this way that Mark already knew of the spill. I also learned that the *Rainbow Whale* had challenged a pirate whaler pursuing a pod of tiny Minke whales. The whales escaped, and the *Rainbow Whale* narrowly missed being rammed. The crew had also stopped hunters from clubbing baby harp seals at the far end of the world, as well as helped cut holes in the ice for two young Gray whales trapped by early winter.

Mark shifted his position, and a new excitement entered his voice. Recently the yellow ship pulled into a city of humans, where she was taken out of the water and new color put on her. There Mark had joined her crew. This was his first voyage on the *Rainbow Whale*, and he took great pride in sailing with others who risked their lives for whales.

Aleea swam up to us. Mark gave a glad cry and splashed over to her. I told him that the two of us had wreathed our spouts together under the moon. He was pleased and climbed up on Aleea's back to speak with her. He told her of the Sargasso Sea and of my pulling him free of it, and I saw by the look in her eye that Aleea understood. She reached over and touched me.

Mark returned to me when Aleea left us, and spoke in low, urgent tones. The pictures that came were perplexing. I saw the *Rainbow Whale* sail far out into the ocean toward a group of islands. Next I saw a fleet of ships like those in the ships' graveyard sail to one of the islands. Men went ashore and built a thing out of trees high into the air, higher than any palm tree. From one of the ships they took a heavy thing made of metal and put it on top of the man-made tree. This metal thing was feared. There was something deadly inside it.

The men left the island and sailed a few miles away. And waited.

For an instant it looked as if the sun fell on that island. A blinding white light filled the sky, brighter than Ohobo's flash. A column of cloud and smoke grew higher than the tallest storm clouds, and I understood. This man-made tree with its metal fruit was like that which many years ago spread fire and cloud over the Waste Sea. And Mark said all this would happen soon.

He showed the island disappear below the waves and all creatures for many leagues die of sickness following the explosion. Clouds filled with poison rained down on the plankton and even on our distant beds of krill. The plankton died, and the krill vanished. Whales who fed on what remained turned belly-up and died.

I was sick at heart.

But then, in a hopeful tone, Mark told me the *Rainbow Whale* planned to sail to the island while the treelike structure was half-built and to stop the men. When I asked how they would stop them, he said he didn't know exactly, but that it would be dangerous. His hope was that the men would take the metal thing back to their ships and sail away.

Last he told me I must lead the pod to the other side of the world and remain there. I protested, but he repeated this urgently several times. It grieved me, though I knew I must do it to guard the pod. Yet what if the other ships caught the *Rainbow Whale* or rammed it and sent it with Mark to the bottom? What if Mark and his friends were near the man-made tree when the evil thing on top of it exploded? It would eat them as it ate the island.

While I carried him back to the *Rainbow Whale*, my heart filled with fear for him. I knew my duty was to go with the scouts to look for the beds of krill and to find a safe course to the far side of the world. But my heart was divided as I thought of Mark's danger—and then I remembered the words spoken to me in the cavern: "*Mark is one of a few who have made the choice. Guard him well.*"

Without a word my friend climbed back on board.

The hull of that little ship seemed very fragile to me, and I felt again the terrible uneasiness that had haunted me over the past weeks. I didn't want to let her out of my sight. But I said nothing while the *Rainbow Whale* started her engines and pulled away from us. The crew called and waved, and the other Humpbacks breached and slapped the water and sang out to them. Mark was as silent as I and waved slowly once.

"May the Whale of Light go with you!" I thought and imagined that brilliant being surrounding the hull of the bravely colored ship.

When it had dropped below the horizon and the others were still, I shared what I'd learned of the danger to the *Rainbow Whale* and to this whole quarter of the ocean. They were alarmed by the news, and we entered into a loud discussion that Hrūna brought to a halt.

"We have little time for words," he said. "To escape such a danger we must immediately seek a way around the ice to the far side of the Pole—perhaps even go to the other End of the World."

We all agreed. But then I told them that I sensed the *Rainbow Whale* and Mark were in immediate danger and that I had decided to follow them. The scouts should go on without me.

"If the *Rainbow Whale* were threatened," Hrūna asked, looking at me closely, "how would you aid her?"

I confessed I didn't know. All I knew was that I had to follow the ship. The others protested, but my mind was made up. Hrūna was silent.

"My son, " he said at last, "this is what I have decided. Aleea and I shall go with you. The others will return to the pod and lead them toward the Pole. When we rejoin them on the way, it will be time enough to scout a passage to the far side of the Pole." Aleea looked relieved.

Without further words, the others returned the way we'd come, while the three of us swam swiftly after the *Rainbow Whale*, which had vanished over the horizon. It was several hours before we caught up with her. When we did, some of the clouds in my mind lifted. The sun shone down, and the yellow ship blazed on a green sea; it was difficult to imagine any harm coming to her. We were careful not to let the crew see us, for fear they'd tell us to go back.

The sun sank, through brilliant layers of orange, red, and purple clouds over a group of islands. The largest island cut a black shape against the western sky. We headed toward the twinkle of tiny lights where a city of humans lay in its shadow. The sails of many small craft glowed in the last light from the west, while anchored in a deep channel between islands loomed the black silhouettes of ships like those in the graveyard. Iron logs bristled from them like spines on a scorpion fish. My uneasiness returned with a pang, for these were the ships Mark had described to me, getting ready to leave on their deadly mission.

That night we floated among the islands, inhaling the rich fragrances of flowers that drifted over the waters, mixed with the smells of burnt oil and dead fish. In the moonlight the cluster of warships floated like enormous sharks with lean, curved jaws. Unlike the city or the smaller craft close in, they showed few lights.

The next morning the *Rainbow Whale* did not leave port. We waited the whole day, worried, hiding behind a reef miles out. Nor did she come out the following morning, and as the second day dragged on, dark clouds again gathered over my thoughts.

The third night dragged even more slowly. In the middle of the night we were awakened by the boom and rattle of anchors weighing. While we watched, the great blind shadows of the war fleet swung west and slid out to sea, moving darkly over waves that glittered like tiny teeth in the moonlight.

When dawn flushed the island pink we saw the bright shape of the *Rainbow Whale* sail proudly out of the harbor. She turned and moved west where the war fleet had weighed anchor. Despite the sun and the ship's brave appearance, the cloud over my thoughts thickened.

I didn't share this feeling with the others but swam closer to the ship than they as she cruised westward among scattered islands. There was no sign of the gray ships, but the *Rainbow Whale* kept steadily on course.

While the sun rose higher, the cloud in my mind grew darker. Sometimes it condensed to a black spot. I swam close to the ship, careless of being seen, almost in her wake. I didn't know what the uneasiness meant, for I hadn't seen any of the sharklike ships on the horizon. Was it that the tree was already built and the metal thing on top would explode before we got there? No. My anxiety was much closer at hand: it focused on Mark and on the *Rainbow Whale*.

I decided to show myself clearly. If Mark was in some new danger, perhaps he knew of it and would tell me. Boldly I breached to port side, but apparently no one was watching. So I crossed in front of the bow and breached as high as I could. The ship veered to starboard and slowed, and Mark appeared on deck, waving his arms wildly and calling. I swam alongside, and he spoke. His voice was stern. He said I should turn back immediately, and he pictured again the fire and cloud and polluting rains. Again he urged me to lead the pod to a new ocean.

In response, I tried to communicate my sense of danger to him. I pictured the *Rainbow Whale* with a black cloud descending on her. I spoke of the sense of dread that pursued her like a giant shark. The trouble was I couldn't name a specific danger. I felt frustrated and foolish.

He nodded and pointed west to the horizon. He said that he understood. He too was worried about the warships that were sure to chase the *Rainbow Whale*. But the little ship was fast, and he counted on her to evade them. Then he walked astern and pointed east, again ordering me to return to the pod. Mark's forehead formed wrinkles, and his mouth flattened to a grim line.

He had not understood. The ship increased her speed.

Swimming close behind, I felt the danger even more acutely. Again I plunged under the ship to breach in front and slow her. When I passed the throbbing screws and the long yellow hull, something black caught my eye. I couldn't remember seeing it before. So I dove back under the ship, rolling to eye the smooth yellow hull, careful to stay well forward of the churning screws.

There was a black thing, metal and round, sticking to the hull like a barnacle but as big around as a stingray. It had not been there the other day when we swam under the ship, the day before the *Rainbow Whale* went into the island harbor. The ship must have picked it up while in the harbor.

I moved close and touched it. I felt a small vibration: *death*.

Instantly I knew death was in that thing. It sang of death. The vibration put a black hole in my thought. In my head I had a clear Seeing of the bowels of the ship bursting into flame. I sensed it would be soon—very soon. Flame and death.

I swam out to port, leaped high in the air and trumpeted *"Death"* to warn them. Mark came to the side of the ship and stared at me.

"Death!" I screamed again, but he shook his head and hunched his flippers. I tried to calm myself as I swam in mad circles about the ship and pictured for him the ship's bowels bursting into flame.

Meanwhile, Hrūna and Aleea heard my warning and were calling to me from a mile back to swim away from the ship. Their cries were as urgent as my own.

Again at the picture of the exploding ship, Mark shook his head and threw up his flippers. I wasn't making the danger clear.

So I swam alongside and pictured very clearly the yellow hull with the black metal barnacle on it. He shook his head. I pictured it again, and still he shook his head and waved his arms.

Then I had an idea.

I dove under the boat and approached the black thing. It put a chill in me.

Keeping up with the ship, I pressed my head against the metal parasite. I heard a faint, rapid clicking at a very high pitch and a tiny vibration smaller than the hull's. It was this I had sensed in the water—that had let me know when I didn't know. It would be soon—the death.

Click, click, click—death, death, death, it sang.

With my flukes I struck the hull next to the black barnacle. I swam up, leaped and returned, banging the hull again. Bellowing, I again pictured for Mark the deadly parasite on the hull.

This time he must have understood what I meant, because he stared at me a moment, his skin a shade whiter, and ran below deck.

Again I dove alongside the black death. *Very soon. Very soon,* the faint vibration sang—*death.* I pushed at it with my flipper, but it stuck to the hull just like a barnacle.

Very soon.

Beside myself, I pushed again, lost my balance, and slipped into the current rushing through the screws. Jerking free, I returned and pushed at it head-on—with no success.

Panicked, I surfaced again. Mark and two others were on deck. All at once the screws stopped, and the boat floated dead in the water.

Very soon. Very soon, the black thing sang louder. I cried to them to hurry, picturing the explosion.

One let down a rope, and Mark and a third were pulling on black skins and tying yellow bladders to their backs. They were slow—too slow. There wasn't time.

"Hurry," I trumpeted, lobtailing. The black thing flashed white in my brain. I banged the hull again, hoping to shake it loose. Pressing my jaw against its narrow edge, I thrust hard, but I only tore my lip and baleen. Ignoring the pain, I pressed again. A cloud of blood blinded me.

Ting, ting, the tiny vibrations sang and *click*—a loud *click.* I knew that the death was only moments away. I heard the splash of men entering the water, but they were slow—slow as in a dream. With the black metal pressing into my jaw, I pushed. The water clouded with blood.

Crack! something gave, and I felt the thing bend away from the hull. It was hanging by one side.

Ting ting whirr CLICK.

With a roar I gave a last ferocious push, and it snapped loose, floating free in the water. The froglike bodies of the two men swam toward me in slow motion. One held a light, and I saw Mark's eyes through glass as it flashed over him.

Ting. The black barnacle turned over in the water, somersaulting slowly—all too slowly—toward the bottom. The men shone the light on it and swam after it.

It was going to go off, and the two would die along with the ship and myself.

Ting. Click click click.

With a bellow I dove between them, seizing it in my jaws. Thrusting violently, I pushed down and away from the hull.

CLICK CLICK CLICK.

The death was about to happen—happen in my mouth.

Down and down. Never had I dived so desperately.

Down and down, the death clicking between my lips.

Down I went—forever, it seemed. Down into the Black Deep.

When it was far enough down, and only then, did I open my mouth and let the Thing drop through the water on its own.

Click-whirr—it sounded.

I turned and kicked upward with all my might. At that instant a flash from behind reflected off the hull far above and I felt a white fire in my bowels. The water squeezed in on me with a deafening roar.

Blackness and a ringing in my head.

I was a fingerling swimming in a dark cave. At the end was a light, and I had to get to the light. But I could move only in a funny waggle, and there was a shark behind that had eaten half of me.

The light in the cave widened. My head cleared and I

was swimming toward the bright surface. I couldn't feel my flukes or the rear half of my body, but I was moving with tremendous speed toward the air. Somehow—though my head was ringing and my lip trailing a dark thread of blood—I had kept my breath when the thing shook the Deep. Brighter and brighter the surface loomed and I saw the yellow hull floating at its center.

Up I shot high into the air, spouting and beating my flippers. The *Rainbow Whale* lay unharmed on the water where I arced over her bow, two white faces staring up at me from the surface. I heard the faint cries of Hrūna and Aleea a mile to the stern.

"I've escaped too," I thought in a brief moment of triumph as I crashed on the far side. But when I rolled over, the lower half of my belly turned red and a dark cloud from it flowed underwater. A fine pink mist rained on me where my spout hung in the air. Suddenly I felt weak, and the *Rainbow Whale* wavered and darkened before my eyes.

Fighting to stay conscious, only now, after the battle, did I sing my battle song, preparing to meet my death:

> *Now I rise from battle, my breath's banner*
> *Bright to behold in the height of the morning.*
> *Hralekana-kolua, on the crest of the comber,*
> *Lifts up his cry to creation's four corners.*
> *Be bold, my breast, as you take the hot steel*
> *Even to the heart where the blood flows brightly.*
> *Say to cow, say to calf in waves yet to come:*
> *He guarded those well who guarded the ocean.*

Chapter Sixteen

THE pain was sudden and sharp. The shock had worn off, and my mind was clear. The *Rainbow Whale* lay still, and a raft from her floated by me where I lay on my side, blood from my belly clouding the water. Mark was beside me, stroking me, making soft choking noises. The others sat silently in the raft or along the rail of the ship.

A mist blew over me as Aleea surfaced and pressed against my back. She fought to hide the panic in her voice as it rose in the ancient comforting words. I felt the warmth of her tears on my back while she sang:

> *Deep in my heart I breathe deeply with you*
> *The breath of the one who made you and keeps you,*
> *The breath of the one whose white wings are healing.*

In the depths appeared a huge shadow, and Hrūna rose on the other side, supporting me and lifting Mark out of the water. Mark crawled over his back onto my head. His speech was broken and slow. Through his words I saw the wound and a piece of steel far inside my body. He kept trying to shut that picture out, but it underlay all he spoke of: our meeting in the pond, our swimming there before I was wounded by the killers, my escape while he watched from shore, and later, our playing together when we met on the high seas. Other memories of our friendship returned—

repeatedly a picture of my swimming and his clinging to my flipper, moving on and on toward a great light.

How long we lay there I cannot tell. The pain in my gut was deep and sharp, and several times I nearly lost consciousness. The pain came and went, and all the while I heard the soft keening of Aleea as she and Hrūna pressed against me, and I saw the words Mark breathed down my blowhole—especially of our swimming and the light growing brighter.

The sun was higher now. Someone called to Mark from the ship, softly at first, then more urgently. I guessed from his tone what he said: they had to sail after the other ships.

It was what they must do.

Stroking me a last time by the blowhole, Mark slid into the water. Still he spoke of our swimming together.

From the ship's rail he sent that picture as he called good-bye. I sang back to him that in my spirit I would swim with the *Rainbow Whale* as she sailed among the gray ships bristling with death. Wherever he went, I said, I would be with him. He raised his flipper in salute, as did the others. The engines coughed and churned, and the ship thrugged slowly off.

Once more I saw him cling to my flipper while we swam toward a light under the sea. Once more I sang to him my promise to be with him. I sang with all the strength I could muster:

> *Wherever on the waters the winds shall find you,*
> *Wherever the moon or the sun shall move,*
> *Hidden in the heavens or splendid high above you,*

Deep in my heart I will breathe deeply with you
The breath of the one who made you and keeps you.

When the ship was a yellow dot on the horizon, Aleea and Hrūna turned me to the east, holding me up on either side.

"Hralekana, my son," Hrūna said. "If only I—" his voice broke off with a squeak, and he pressed hard against me. Both were quiet while they slowly, with infinite patience, helped me along. Speaking in low tones, they set a course to find the others migrating toward the Pole.

That was a long day in the sun. I could move my flukes, but at each thrust I felt pain. While the day wore on, I could feel the steel fragment move in my gut and it worried me. The sun was hot, and often we'd stop while I sank under a moment. But the water felt cold—too cold for the tropics. My breath was tinged with blood.

We didn't dare pause for long. We were moving at a crawl, and the bleeding continued. In uneasy, feverish fits I dreamt we were followed. Too cold, too hot, the day inched past.

"Look back there," Hrūna whispered during one of our rests. A number of fins, some white, some gray, circled at a distance behind us. The scent of my blood was strong in the water, for no matter what Hrūna or Aleea did, the sharks would not scare. At last the two called out a distress signal, aiming it along the ocean floor.

That night the moon was full, and though I needed rest badly, the others said we must swim. The silhouettes of the trailing fins moved closer and encircled us. Gradually they tightened the circle. Maddened by the taste of blood, the sharks were losing their fear.

I was blacking out briefly from the pain, though I didn't tell the others. An hour after moonrise a shadow flashed under me. It was a large white making a pass at my wound. I lurched ahead. Hrūna saw it and sank under me. The shark circled and returned, crazed by the scent. When it passed, Hrūna twisted in one convulsive motion. There was a squelch of flesh against flesh and the trumpet of an angry whale. The shark erupted from the water, landing with an enormous splash. I glimpsed its crooked shadow fleeing toward the horizon.

"That's only one," Hrūna said, rising. "The others will try now." Hrūna and Aleea signaled again, and we heard a whisper pass through the water—a faint chorus of silvery whistles. The pod was scores of miles distant, but the trace of their voices comforted me.

By ones and twos the other sharks attacked. Hrūna and Aleea fended them off but were slowly losing strength. The marauders grew bolder and circled just out of reach. I had long since ceased to care.

Midnight came and passed. I was about to tell the others to go on without me when silver geysers erupted on the horizon, followed by a thunder of flukes striking the water. To a fin, the sharks turned and fled.

I must have lapsed unconscious then, because when I opened my eyes, the whole pod surrounded me. Hrūna was explaining what had happened, and I saw floating before me, as if in a dream, the faces of Hrunta and Hreelëa.

Then I saw the face of my mother Lewtë up close. She was in anguish. She insisted the others move away and rose under me, holding me up as she did when I was a calf—though she was now only half my size. I worried I was too heavy for her, but her head surfaced under the wound and she raised it above the water. I saw her expression as the dark blood streaked down her face. She gave a cry that I had never heard from a whale, even one mortally wounded—as if a harpoon had pierced her through from mouth to flukes.

Others came and took her from me. Hrūna called a meeting of the Council close by. They talked for a long time, while I faded in and out of consciousness. At last Hrūna came up to me, his voice subdued, repeatedly clearing his throat. His face was a dark shadow.

"Hralekana-kolua," he said, using my full name, "we are at a loss. Aleea has told us of the deep healing fires, but they are half a world away. We do not know what to do, and have come for your advice."

Hazy as I was, the pain kept my wits clear. I knew what I must do, and I was ready to tell him.

"Take me to Hralekana's cavern," I said calmly.

"What?" Hrūna asked, stunned.

"To Hralekana's cavern." I repeated.

"Alas, you cannot go there," he said sadly, as if he thought I were delirious. "You are seriously wounded. You would never live through the dive."

"Nevertheless, I must go there," I replied.

He gave me a long, searching look.

At last Hrūna glanced down and made a strange clearing sound in his throat.

"Listen!" he called out to the others. "Listen to me, all whales of the pod." The others swam up silently, even the calves.

"It is Hralekana's solemn wish to go to the cavern of his namesake. Aleea, Lewtë, and others, together with myself, will take him there. Scouts will go behind and before to protect us and to honor his name. The rest of the pod will take the calves and young ones and swim with haste toward the Ice at the End of the World."

All were silent, but all obeyed. So, with Lewtë and Aleea bearing me up, and others around us in a circle, we swam off from the pod down the brilliant track of the moon pointing toward Hralekana's cavern. I was hazy, and much that passed from that time on had a dreamlike quality about it. We were borne along by a current of music from behind, while those with me were silent. The current swelled and sank, wild and sweet, a melody from an ancient song about days gone by:

> Fresh as the first beam glittering on a fin
> That brings our friends up from the underworld,
> Sad as the last that reddens over one
> Who sinks with all we love below the verge,
> So sad, so fresh, the days that are no more.

We had gone but a little way when we heard the voices of the whole pod rise in chorus and turned to watch the bright geysers of water where they breached in farewell. Their words rang clearly over the waves:

Hralekana-kolua who have given your heartsblood,
Great will your honor be, high your renown,
For you took in your mouth the murderous steel
And plunged to the depths that it not destroy dear ones,
In your own belly taking its bite and its fire,
For man and whale and the least sea creature—
Saving the ship that may yet save the ocean
From a dark and deadly invisible death.

Feebly I sang back:

Surely as the sun swims after the moon,
So does my heart press hard after yours.
Though my flukes fly as far as the Pole,
My soul sails to you as if to its center.

The rest of our journey is a blur, except that slowly, with many pauses, I sang to the others the song of my life, beginning with my birth and bringing it up to the present—knowing that it would sink into the pool of their memory and they would later recall each note. I knew I had to finish my song and I fought to stay awake and to keep my mind from wandering.

Yet some of my pauses turned into long breaks in the narrative whenever I faded and grew delirious. One of my strongest impressions at the time was that we were not alone. I recall opening my eyes under a moon-bright sea, the waves glittering like scales before us. Off to the side I glimpsed a human face. I blinked, and it rose again, eyes wild and hair streaming behind it. And then, another and another, their human flippers beckoning to me. They swam parallel to us, and one cradled a shell in his arms. No one else appeared to see them, and I was about to cry out when I heard the singing, the ravishing singing, fade in and out of the waves:

O come to us here, where land and sea marry,
The wanderer's rest, and the wild wave's.
The bitter cold sea and the hot sun above you
Will no longer burn where our bright hair floats over you.

Land and sea, sun and moon, day and night, storm and calm,
Depth and height, cold and heat, light and dark, wound and balm,
Marry in the music that murmurs like a river
Where we swim in our bright golden caverns forever.

Their voices, hypnotic and sweet, made me want to give over this painful journey and to sink to the cool deep below, and I wondered if I shouldn't close my ears against them. A stab of pain in my side forced me to shut my eyes, and when I opened them, the sweet singers were gone—though all that night their voices echoed in my head whenever I fell into delirium. I recalled Aleea's vision of the beauty and peril of the mermen and mermaids, and I remembered their singing on our wedding night, which now seemed so long ago.

226

I don't know how much time passed, but it was dawn of the next day—or the next—that we came to those waters I knew so well. Even through the growing brightness of the dawn, as the stars winked out we read our position and knew we were above Hralekana's cavern.

The faces of the others in that early light looked gray with despair. We lay there, the small waves slapping against flipper and fluke in that draining light. The scouts had come in, and we huddled, rising and falling together in the soft swell.

I had brought my story up to that moment, even as we paused. The effort of it and the journey had left me very weak. I husbanded my remaining strength.

No one spoke.

Weak as I was, and in pain, I knew I could—I must—dive down to the cavern underneath. Slowly I said good-bye to Hrunta and Hreelëa, then Hrūna and Lewtë, and last, Aleea. As I hugged them, I whispered a word in each one's ear.

Aleea and I clung to each other a long time. I whispered to her, and then we said nothing. Nothing more could be said. I felt the slow beat of her heart next to mine.

When the sun rose, tingeing the mist pink, I turned and gave each a last look.

Throwing my flukes high in the air, I plunged. Down with every ounce of my remaining strength I dove, and I felt the Deep close about me, pressing the wound into my side. The pain was so great I thought I'd break in two. Down into the terrible pressure, the squidlike dark, I delved. Down I struggled, until I saw the dim light of the cave far below. I swam for it hard, clenching my jaws to keep from crying out. Then the entrance was before me. With a last thrust of my flukes, I was inside.

It was as I had left it. Still and silent, each rock undisturbed, glowing dimly. In the light I saw a small thread of blood uncurling from my wound. At this depth the pain had subsided and was quite bearable. Despite my exertions, I felt strengthened. As in past times, I felt no deprivation of breath. Facing the dark opening, thinking of the friends I left on the surface—they would still be there, wondering, not yet sharing with each other what I had said to each, the sun rising in all its glory over the waves, turning the mist to gold—I began intoning the word.

Over and over I said it, louder and louder, feeling my strength increase, till I knew its resonance carried it upward to those waiting. I knew they heard it, and confused perhaps, each glanced at the other as the gold light flooded their faces, a wild hope exploding in each heart.